Music Discovery

Improvisation for the Large Ensemble and Music Classroom

Daniel J. Healy

AND

Kimberly Lansinger Ankney

OXFORD
UNIVERSITY PRESS

OXFORD
UNIVERSITY PRESS

Oxford University Press is a department of the University of Oxford. It furthers
the University's objective of excellence in research, scholarship, and education
by publishing worldwide. Oxford is a registered trade mark of Oxford University
Press in the UK and certain other countries.

Published in the United States of America by Oxford University Press
198 Madison Avenue, New York, NY 10016, United States of America.

Library of Congress Cataloging-in-Publication Data
Names: Healy, Daniel J., author. | Ankney, Kimberly Lansinger author.
Title: Music discovery : improvisation for the large ensemble and
music classroom / Daniel J. Healy and Kimberly Lansinger Ankney.
Description: New York : Oxford University Press, 2020. |
Includes bibliographical references and index.
Identifiers: LCCN 2019041870 (print) | LCCN 2019041871 (ebook) |
ISBN 9780190462062 (hardback) | ISBN 9780190462079 (paperback) |
ISBN 9780190462093 (epub)
Subjects: LCSH: Improvisation (Music) | Music—Instruction and study.
Classification: LCC MT68 .H416 2020 (print) | LCC MT68 (ebook) |
DDC 781.3/6—dc23
LC record available at https://lccn.loc.gov/2019041870
LC ebook record available at https://lccn.loc.gov/2019041871

9 8 7 6 5 4 3 2 1

Paperback printed by Marquis, Canada
Hardback printed by Bridgeport National Bindery, Inc., United States of America

First and foremost, I would like to thank my beautiful wife, Abigail, and our two sons, Thomas and Owen. Abigail, your unfaltering support made this project possible. Thomas and Owen, your imaginative and often hilarious play constantly reminds me of why I love teaching improvisation. My endlessly generous mom and dad, my entire wonderful family, and all the invaluable music teachers and mentors in my life.
~ Dan

Thank you, Matt, for all your support in this large writing project!! Ethan, Aaron, and Evelyn—your personalities and laughter have inspired me to improvise in life and music!! Thank you also to my parents and many music mentors who have fostered a love of music in me that has lasted a lifetime!
~ Kim

Contents

SECTION III   Lessons

Acknowledgments

Both authors would like to offer profound thanks to the following individuals: Norm Hirschy for his brilliant editing and considerable patience with this large project, Lauralee Yearly for her valuable assistance. Our mentor, Maud Hickey, for introducing us to the scholarly world of improvisation; Janet Barrett; Peter Webster; all of our colleagues who supported our initial work through the Center for the Study of Education and the Musical Experience at Northwestern University; Susan Conkling, who is gone but not forgotten; Matt Turner; David Berkman; Jeffrey Albert; Chris Madsen; David Kay; Butch Marshall; Alex Marshall; Terry Riley; Andrew Stein-Zeller; Tom Welsh; Anthony Braxton; Kyoko Kitamura; and the folks at the Tricentric Foundation, the Pauline Oliveros estate, Al Margolis, Ione, Pat Harbison, and Mike Kanan for providing access to invaluable musical resources.

Nicholas Conner, Kelly Rossum, Miles Comiskey, Marty Kalas, Scott Stickley, Louise O'Hanlon, Anissa Jody, Michael Velasquez, and their wonderful students for recording musical examples of this book's activities.

About the Companion Website

www.oup.com/us/musicdiscovery

Oxford University Press has created a website to accompany this book. This website includes recorded examples of some of the book's lesson activities by school ensembles and music classes.

We would like to remind the reader that each recording is meant as an audio example of a lesson activity procedure, not an archetype. Teachers and students should not be discouraged if their version of an activity sounds different than the recording; this is the nature of improvisation. Some lessons have several component parts such as *Rhythmic Mash-Up* and *Prayer Meeting from Outer Space.* For these lessons teachers will find audio tracks featuring each requisite part.

Melody

1.1 "Brahmsian Improvisation," Herricks High School Wind Ensemble, Director: Scott Stickley
2.1 "Middle Eastern Taqsim" teacher model, String Workshop
2.2 "Middle Eastern Taqsim" student example, String Workshop

Harmony

3.1 "Mood Music," Fairview South Elementary School Band, Director: Nicholas Conner
4.1 "Celestial Navigation," Herricks High School Chamber Choir, unison, Director: Louise O'Hanlon

Rhythm

Texture and Timbre

Articulation

Dynamics

11.1 Studio Magic, Lane Tech College Prep High School Music Theory Class, Project 1, Director: Miles Comiskey

11.2 Studio Magic, Lane Tech College Prep High School Music Theory Class, Project 2, Director: Miles Comiskey

11.3 Studio Magic, Lane Tech College Prep High School Music Theory Class, Project 3, Director: Miles Comiskey

* Mrs. Carter and Warren High School are pseudonyms for a high school in the eastern United States.

Improvisation in the Large Ensemble and Classroom

Introduction

Spontaneity is the moment of personal freedom when we are faced with a
reality and see it, explore it and act accordingly.
  —V. Spolin (1999, p. 4)

Improvisation is spontaneity in music. It can be beautiful, uplifting, and unnerving all
at the same time. It happens instantaneously, in a unique context, with ideas never to be
performed the same way again. It can be the result of years of practice or an unexpected
reaction to a collaborative musical moment. As Spolin so eloquently explains, it provides
musicians with an opportunity to explore a musical situation in which boundaries can
be stretched and new ideas can be enacted. Out of these experiences comes a sense of
freedom and agency that can inspire a young musician. We have seen the power of these
experiences in our own students, and we hope to foster those same experiences for students through the teaching approaches and activities discussed in this book.

Where do improvised musical moments live in the typical music curriculum? We
know that it is a challenge to incorporate improvisation on a consistent basis. As new
music teachers, we often incorporated improvisation as a culminating experience at the
end of a unit, or we saved improvisation experiences until concerts were completed.
Improvisation did not seem like something that we could address year long when the
demands of content or performance were so great. It changed our teaching when we realized that we could integrate music improvisation activities consistently into the ensemble
or music classroom curriculum. Furthermore, we realized that we did not need to hit the
"pause" button on concert preparation to work on an improvisation unit; both repertoire
and improvisation could advance our students' performance abilities.

A music teacher can do this in a group setting by tapping into students' diverse
personalities and voices. Improvisation is often framed as an independent enterprise,
but an eclectic group of students provides boundless opportunities for rich and varied
musical collaboration. Moreover, the teacher can be essential in facilitating vibrant
group improvisation experiences. There is something different that happens in musical

development when we set up opportunities for students to make spontaneous musical choices for themselves. Students begin to listen differently, watch differently, respond differently, and perform differently if we give them the space to stretch musical boundaries and create their own musical ideas.

How do we know that students change when they begin to improvise? By focusing on musical elements in improvised activities such as melody, harmony, rhythm, timbre/texture, articulation, and dynamics consistently over time—we have seen students transform. By focusing on these musical elements, students can begin to connect and produce music that reflects layered levels of musical understanding. Furthermore, when lessons are exploratory, interdisciplinary, or inspired by principles in various genres, students will experience more fluid musical interactions, become more attuned to their neighbors, and be more open and adaptive to musical ideas.

This book is designed to provide an accessible approach to including musical improvisation in the large ensemble and classroom setting. It is chiefly based on the transformative musical experiences we have had with students when we began incorporating improvisation into our teaching. The spontaneous and unpredictable nature of musical improvisation can be challenging, but the rewards far outweigh any momentary trepidation that teachers and students might feel. The pedagogical suggestions and lesson plans presented will make the benefits of teaching and learning improvisation clear and provide an approach that is adaptable and manageable for music teachers working with large numbers of students. In doing so, teachers will learn more about students' musical thinking and will enhance musicianship skills for their entire ensembles.

The 2014 National Music Standards call for music teachers to engage students in the musical process of creation and describes improvisation as an integral experience. Yet we know many teachers, particularly in large ensembles and classroom settings, still struggle to find ways to make improvisation a reality (Bernhard, 2013; Bernhard & Stringham, 2016; Schopp, 2006). The book is framed around practical and flexible ideas for implementing improvisation activities. The lesson activities borrow broad principles from different musical styles and genres to provide a variety of improvisation settings and appeal to diverse student interests. Many activities are exploratory in nature, allowing students to play and respond to one another while also focusing on core musical elements such as melody and rhythm. Interdisciplinary teaching approaches and resources are suggested throughout many of the lessons to enhance creative expression and build connections between the arts. Lessons include learning objectives, detailed procedures, assessments, benefits, recordings, and MP3 examples.

How to Use This Book

This book is specifically designed with an appreciation for today's busy music teacher. If you are anything like the music teachers we know, you are among the busiest people in your school. You handle performances, curriculum planning, adjudications, managerial responsibilities, and everyday responsibilities of responding to the students. Many music teachers seek to enrich students' musical lives through creative experiences but this task can be challenging when teachers are standing in front of a large music classroom or ensemble. This volume does not ask the reader to throw out curriculum or discard practices developed by the teacher. The reader is not encouraged to scrap the concert band in favor of an improvisation ensemble or have raga activities replace valuable Kodaly lessons in the general music classroom. Instead, the resources in this text can be integrated into existing curriculum to meet and enhance the goals of the music classroom. Moreover, the reader should not feel compelled to fully diverge from his or her regular teaching practices, particularly those that reflect the teacher's personal interests. The purpose of this book is to flexibly frame improvisation activities in a way that allows the busy music teacher to "streamline" or integrate valuable improvisation experiences into their regular music teaching activities.

How Can I Get Students to Improvise?

How does one learn improvisation? The only answer is to ask another question: What is stopping us?
—S. NACHMANOVITCH (1991, p. 10)

It is amazing how many people we encounter who say, "I'm not an improviser." The more that we discuss this topic with music teachers, the more it becomes apparent that they are not *really* saying, "I'm not an improviser." They are saying, "I cannot play fluidly over bebop chord changes," or "I do not know anything about improvised world music styles." Keep in mind that none of these statements means the same thing as "I'm not an improviser." One of the profound joys of teaching so many improvisation lessons and participating in so many professional development sessions is the realization that any musical activity can be framed as an entry point to improvisation. We love the look on participants' faces when they perform an activity modeled after minimalist composition, where their only improvisational prompt is to determine how many times each phrase should be repeated. Many have a look that seems to say, "That's it?! That's improvising?" The answer is an unequivocal *yes* because any form of spontaneously expressed musical ideas is improvisation. Soloing over John Coltrane's "Giant Steps" at a breakneck tempo is improvisation, but so is playing a major scale with a malleable tempo. The general purpose of this book is to provide flexible entry points to improvisation for *all* music teachers and students.

It is intriguing to us when we encounter *teachers* who say they are not improvisers, because, as education writers such as Elliot Eisner (2002), Maxine Greene (1978), and Keith Sawyer (2004) have noted, teaching is one of the most improvisational professions in existence. The ability to connect topical lessons to a group of diverse, dynamic children or adolescents requires substantial improvisational skill. Keith Sawyer

(2004), a distinguished researcher on creativity, notes that the classroom often mirrors the "collaborative emergence" of improvisational theater. He writes that "[b]oth class-room discussion and theater improvisations are *emergent* because the outcome cannot be predicted in advance, and they are *collaborative* because no single participant can con-trol what emerges; the outcome is collectively determined by all participants" (p. 13). Music teaching can require even more improvisation because the teacher must process and navigate real-time sound production and performance. Because of this requirement, we believe that teachers are well poised to be the facilitators of musical improvisation ex-periences, and that students will embrace these experiences when teachers take the first step to include improvisation activities in the music classroom. Together, musical ideas will emerge that will surprise and support the existing music curriculum.

What Is the Purpose of This Book?

1. The book provides improvisation activities for teachers working with many students in large ensembles and classrooms.

   Music teachers understand that the larger the group of students, the more un-wieldy the interaction of student dynamics. It is one of the reasons that many educa-tion policy advocates encourage smaller classrooms. Some music teachers worry that, if they let a group of that size improvise, it will result in noise or cacophony. Others might think, "These students are experienced only in singing/playing the notes that are on the page; they will panic if I ask them to improvise." This book is intended to provide flexible entry points to activities that are designed for large music classrooms whether it be for the ensemble, general music, or other settings. The lessons are de-signed for different levels of learners, including beginner, intermediate, and advanced students. Furthermore, the lessons outline a number of different improvisation "ex-periences." Several prompt the students to improvise with specific passages from their repertoire, an activity that can help ease the teacher and the students into improvisa-tion, while others may stretch students' musical boundaries when the teacher deems it appropriate.

2. The lessons are centered around key music learning principles (melody, harmony, rhythm, texture/timbre, articulation, dynamics) so that they can streamline into broader student learning.

   In a way, this point dovetails into the previous time management concern of many music teachers. Some teachers worry that time spent on improvisation will take away from the requisite musical skills needed for the students to give a quality performance. The performances or products of an ensemble or class are undoubtedly connected to the specific music knowledge and skills learned by the students. Music teachers use as-sessment and feedback to gauge where students require musical improvement: for ex-ample, an orchestra that plays well in simple meter but struggles in compound meter. As a means of helping students grow musically, this book's improvisation activities are framed around *six* music learning skills. It is organized in this way so that the teacher can use these activities to address certain learning needs that are identified by assessment or performance. In this way, the teacher can select improvisation lessons that streamline musical growth for a class. Using the previous time signature example, the teacher can prompt the orchestra to participate in a lesson that allows the students to practice and develop awareness in compound meter. This musical growth will then amplify the students' ability to perform and experience different types of music.

3. The book provides teachers with detailed lessons.

   Many music teachers may wonder, "I want to do improvisation with my students but what do I do? Where do I even start?" This is an understandable concern, as Nachmanovitch (1991) notes: "if you have all of the colors available, you are sometimes almost too free. With one dimension constrained, play becomes freer in other dimensions" (p. 85). This book, in turn, provides detailed activities that focus on particular "dimensions" of musical improvisation. The activities are presented in a lesson plan format familiar to most teachers, including learning goals, procedures, and assessments. The lessons include detailed procedures, often with several options so that a teacher can approach the activity with clarity while also catering the lesson to the unique student dynamics of his or her class. Several of the lessons also have interdisciplinary connections that can enhance students' understandings across the arts.

4. The lessons are flexibly designed so that they will not take time away from concert preparation.

   For many music teachers, ensemble concerts provide a valuable opportunity to provide students, parents, other teachers, and the community with a performance or product that is reflective of class activities and progress. Conversely, many teachers also cite concert or contest deadlines as one of the more stressful aspects of music teaching. Some teachers express that they do not have enough time with their students for quality concert preparation and that is the reason that some of these teachers do not engage their classes in improvisation activities. Class time is a precious commodity for teachers and this is an understandable concern. With such issues in mind, the lessons in this book were flexibly designed so that the teacher can dedicate either five minutes or an hour of class time to the activity. Many of the lessons are *process oriented*, allowing the teacher to focus on ongoing musical growth instead of a scrutinized product. Many can be used as a simple warm-up, while some can be used in actual performances, if the teacher so desires.

5. The lessons provide teachers with detailed assessments.

   If we take this point further, many in the profession often wonder how to assess their students on improvisation, particularly if the improvisation is creative, idiomatic, and personal. This book provides a distinct focus on assessment in conjunction with the presented lessons. Multiple assessment options are presented for each activity and they cover a number of dimensions, including formative assessment methods (in which ongoing feedback is given) and summative assessment methods (in which final evaluations/grades are given). The spectrum of assessments is presented with the intent of providing a number of different ways that both the teacher and students can experience valuable feedback and subsequent growth.

6. The lessons provide suggested recordings and MP3 examples for lessons.

Since music is aurally experienced, it can be disorienting for a music teacher to teach from a written lesson plan without an aural model. This book includes both a list of recommended recordings that illustrate the musical dimensions of the lesson and a companion website with recordings of real student ensembles performing some activities. The recommended recordings are useful in that they provide archetypal examples of artist-level musicians performing and improvising with the given dimensions of the stated lesson. However, since nearly all of the cited recordings were performed without the stated lesson in mind, the companion website recordings provide actual student-performed versions of the activities that teachers and students can consult in conjunction with a given lesson's written procedure.

Why Improvisation?

Maud Hickey (2012) notes, "Although we can rightfully boast about North America's vast success in producing phenomenal school bands, orchestras and choirs, and professional-level-performance musicians who have come through the ranks of these school programs ever since the inception of school music education in the 1800s, we are probably the least successful when it comes to teaching the art of music creation through improvisation and composition" (p. 1). Few would argue with "North America's vast success in producing phenomenal school bands, orchestras and choirs." Why then, one might ask, is musical improvisation important for students when time is such a limited commodity? It is an important question and we attempt to answer that in this subsection.

A. Improvisation allows students to approach problem solving in a uniquely spontaneous way.

Problem-solving is an integral part of teacher and learner growth. Music, in all of its forms, presents many rich opportunities for problem solving and student growth. The unique affordance of musical improvisation is that the spontaneous, emergent quality of improvisation presents problems previously unknown to the student. For example, a virtuosic first-chair trumpeter in a school wind ensemble might play the melody with a brilliant sound and execution, but how well does that same student adjust to the dynamic blend of an improvisation ensemble? If the student does not blend in an improvisation ensemble with the same confidence, does that response shine a light on the need to listen more to larger ensemble textures? A brilliant concert pianist may play a Mozart concerto to perfection, but how well can that pianist improvise a cadenza within the work (in point of fact, the common practice of Mozart's time)? If the student expertly performs a written cadenza but panics at the notion of an improvised cadenza, what does that anxiety say about the student's ability to intelligently manipulate the musical elements of that cadenza? What does that say about the student's ability to apply melodic, harmonic, and rhythmic skills and knowledge in novel scenarios. Moreover, would such abilities enrich all areas of the pianist's musical performance? In our mind, the answer is a definitive *yes*.

B. Musical improvisation allows students to shift, organize, modify, and transform musical elements in personal ways.

Musical improvisation draws students in because it can be playful and exploratory in nature. It allows students to reconceive musical elements in their terms. The inestimable value of this process is obvious in young children but is often lost on adults and adolescents, who are accustomed to routines and traditions. Beyond the obvious fun of play, such play or exploration possesses rich learning opportunities because it allows the student to investigate the possibilities and boundaries of things, unencumbered by rigid expectations. Ironically, it is likely that *all* established musical techniques and practices were the end result of exploration, as nobody was born knowing the correct violin performance practice or the correct way to harmonize a chorale. For example, if a flute student explores intonation by bending a pitch up and down, that student will develop a greater awareness of the scope and possibilities of flute intonation, regardless of whether the student ends up playing A = 440 perfectly. The ability to transform musical elements enhances the student's awareness and skill in *all* those musical qualities.

C. Music improvisation allows students to develop a sense of *self* or *identity* in the presence of spontaneity.

> The intuitive can only respond in immediacy—right now. It comes bearing its gifts in the moment of spontaneity . . . through spontaneity we are re-formed into ourselves. It creates an explosion that for the moment frees us from handed-down frames of reference, memory choked with old facts and information and undigested theories and techniques of other people's findings. Spontaneity is the moment of personal freedom when we are faced with a reality and see it, explore it and act accordingly.
>
> —*V. Spolin (1999, p. 4)*

As Viola Spolin notes, spontaneity can be a very liberating expression of identity for young students. More recently, the education field is becoming more attuned to the powerful influence of social-emotional learning. Students are unique, dynamic individuals, not vessels for music performance. When music teachers develop and teach *to* such personal dynamics, it paves the way for students to grow personally *and* musically. Musical improvisation requires such spontaneity in that there is no time for a student to consult "handed-down frames of reference" and, in the process, tells the student something valuable about themselves. This is where the teacher can be an essential part of communication. Music teachers can frame friendly, exploratory environments where students can be themselves musically and spontaneously interact with other students. The teacher can do so by encouraging students to do what comes naturally, to try things out and make mistakes (Healy, 2014). This can be a refreshing practice for students whose school experience often prompts them to get the correct answer or face a grade deduction. In particular, the music teacher is in a position to take in feedback and give suggestions on the basis of the group dynamics of a given performance. In a group-improvisation setting, the teacher can suggest logistical changes that do not require any student to completely alter his or her individual approach. Examples include suggesting students alternately play and rest, adjusting the seating of the ensemble, or encouraging students to listen to a different section of the group.

Benefits

Activities in this book encourage fundamental music exploration and often utilize or combine different musical genres or cultures. By its very nature, group improvisation takes spontaneous, unexpected turns, which are not bound by a musical score or genre concept. Because of this quality, teachers sometimes find that new student leaders come to the forefront, displaying their underlying musical understandings in a way that was not possible in the traditional ensemble or classroom setting. In the process, the flexibility of these activities gives students in-the-moment individual autonomy, and their choices reflect their musical perceptions. At one moment a student may play a melodic line on the violin but in the next hear a secondary melody in the bass and shift from the violin's traditional melodic role to accompanying the bass with chopped percussive bowing. As students take on these roles, and rotate through them, they are learning to listen more closely, collaborate intentionally, and create in ways that are meaningful to the ensemble and audiences. These experiences broaden students' perceptions of traditional musical roles.

Advantages for Students

Participation in large ensembles and class music settings affords students the opportunity to immerse themselves in experiential learning, a type of learning that is far richer than pure fact and figure rote learning. This point is true whether our students are performing a mass, learning a march for an upcoming parade, or rehearsing for an assessed performance. In many of these traditional settings, the teacher most often directs the musical choices and the students play out those choices through their musical interactions. However, through improvisation students' experiential learning can be enhanced and they can expand their ownership in musical decision-making.

Students can heighten their understanding of melody, harmony, rhythm, theory (scales/chords), blend, articulation, dynamics, texture, and timbre all through repertoire-aligned improvisation activities. There are endless exploration activities that can refine students' overall musicianship as well as relate to repertoire and musical issues in ensemble performance. Improvisation allows students to distribute musical decision-making across the ensemble and provides space for students to discover what works best in the process of music-making, and what works best for the collaborative performance. In the process of improvisation, students discover the nuanced give and take that happens between performers. These skills move beyond notes, rhythms, and harmonies and include collaboration, spontaneity, and careful listening and responding. The musical performance that is a result of flexible and exploratory improvisation can often differ from what students typically hear and feel through Western classical music experiences in traditional ensembles. The flexibility to produce a work that is less bound by genre or repertoire allows students to personally explore the musical elements that make music emotionally fulfilling for them. Making these in-the-moment choices is empowering for students, as illustrated by a quotation from one of our former students. She wrote, "I had often felt inadequate in my musical instrument capabilities because of my difficulties sight reading and therefore playing classical music. This [group improvisation] class has redefined what it means to excel in music." And excel she did, her final project was a remarkable concert in which she improvised vocal melodies and lyrics over common guitar chord progressions. Her experiences in and through improvisation led her back to herself as a musician. *By no means is this meant to criticize the school ensembles that did not appeal to this student. Different school music ensembles allow countless students to discover and experience music every day.* The important takeaway from this student's statement is that musical improvisation is but one way to expand students' qualitative experiences and, hopefully, an additional way to help them discover and appreciate their unique musical personalities.

In group improvisation, the feedback and improvement processes are unique in that musical goals are often fleeting in nature. Unlike in a musical ensemble that is working from the same score, students may enter a group improvisation with similar broad musical goals but, as spontaneous and unexpected musical events occur in the improvisation, the students' goals may change midstream. These changes offer opportunities for problem finding, identifying issues that do not align with predetermined goals. Furthermore, students benefit from engaging in the problem-solving process. Students come to these decisions when given space for their own post-performance discussion and, when needed, through teacher prompts. Students can further engage in problem finding and problem solving when improvising groups are asked to listen to one another. It is powerful to have groups describe their perceptions of an improvisation performance and to identify what worked or did not work within a performance. When moments for critical reflection are built into improvisation experiences, students will feel agency in the creative process and ownership over the creative product.

Advantages for Teachers

Noticing student growth through improvisation activities is a personally rewarding experience for teachers, but there are added benefits to teacher practice that are just as important and sustaining to teachers' professional development. As teachers include improvisation activities in the music classroom, there is a shift in their positioning within that setting. They are no longer able to teach with as much direct control. While this concept may be intimidating at first, through improvisation, teachers become more attuned to students' natural music-making instincts. They can step aside, listen, probe student thinking, and redesign ways to engage students' musical thinking and performance abilities. Sawyer (2004) describes this interaction between teachers and students during improvisation as *collaborative emergence*, a phrase borrowed from improvisational theater. It is an in-the-moment type of teaching that requires teachers to pause, listen, and engage as participants.

To some, this type of teaching may appear a bit haphazard, disorganized, or short sighted. How can a teacher plan effectively for classes when she is constantly teaching on the basis of moment-to-moment experiences? We certainly do not recommend that a music teacher discard the invaluable practice of lesson planning. Many veteran teachers observe that masterful teaching in any area is a delicate dance between lesson planning and emergent events in the classroom. Improvisation is a micro-version of what music teachers must handle on a larger and more expansive scale in traditional ensembles. Ensemble teachers plan rehearsals carefully on the basis of a musical score but on the basis of these plans, they spontaneously listen, respond, rehearse, and then plan appropriate goals for the next lesson. With teaching improvisation, a similar listening and response pattern occurs but there is no objective score to reference. Instead, teachers are forced to listen deeply and consider the multileveled understandings of all of their students. More simply, teaching improvisation can help teachers with their ability to listen, respond, and engage meaningfully with students on a day-to-day basis.

Arts education philosopher Elliot Eisner (2002) studied the perspectives and approaches of teachers in the visual arts. He observed that "artistry in teaching is more likely to occur when the classroom provides a context for improvisation and where unpredictability, rather than predictability of activities and consequences, is acknowledged" (p. 152). Eisner observed that the "artistry" of teaching happens when teachers allow for the spontaneous "give and take" that is embodied in improvisation. This approach requires that the teacher and students embrace a musical outcome that is less secure in the near future. But together, there is a reliance on one another to achieve something better. This pursuit of excellence by engaged and active students as well as committed teachers leads to stronger musicianship for all.

Popular Myths Concerning Improvisation Pedagogy

Improvisation enjoys the curious distinction of being both the most widely practiced of all musical activities and the least acknowledged and understood. While it is today present in almost every area of music, there is an almost total absence of information about it.
    —D. Bailey (1992, p. ix)

In our experience teaching improvisation, we have encountered some pervasive myths about the teaching and learning of improvisation. In our experience, "buying in" to these myths can create anxiety about teaching improvisation. For music teachers who wish to incorporate improvisation into their classrooms, it is important to place these myths in context so that they can pursue rich improvisation activities without hesitation or misgivings.

The next section presents a list of popular myths that teachers may have heard, or may hear as they embark on a journey teaching improvisation. We attempt to address these myths head on, framing the discussion around research, performance artists, and our experience, in order to encourage educators to explore improvisation as a skill that can broaden students' musicianship.

Popular Myths Concerning Improvisation

Improvisation Is "Unteachable"

Response: The history of improvisation pedagogy reveals countless improvisation teaching and learning success stories. The lasting pedagogical influence of jazz legends Clark Terry and Barry Harris have been well documented (Berliner, 1994) as has the impact of many Hindustani "gurus" in India (Bailey, 1992). Group improvisation teachers such as John

Stevens, Ed Sarath, Fred Frith, Matt Turner, Pauline Oliveros, and David Ballou have successfully integrated novice improvisers for decades (Bailey, 1992; Hickey, 2009). Musical improvisation is just as "teachable" as basketball, pastry baking, fly fishing, or any other skilled activity. Teaching any complex activity involves a combination of learned skills and spontaneous interaction. Boundaries exist to be explored in all disciplines. Teachers can monitor the opening and stretching of these boundaries in music improvisation in a manner similar to a basketball coach who frames practice scenarios so that players will use their developed skills successfully in a spontaneous game situation. The teacher can "teach" improvisation by changing the boundaries of the musical game so that musical concepts are explored, come into focus, and then are refined over time. Furthermore, a music teacher who frames an environment that encourages student exploration and group listening provides fertile ground for student improvisation growth.

Improvisation Is a Purely Mystical/Spiritual/Ethereal Effort That Cannot Be Quantified for Teaching.

Response: Anybody can improvise and, more importantly, anybody can improve at improvisation through practice and exploration. Most improvisation scholarship backs up that every person can improvise (Bailey, 1992; Berliner, 1994; Hickey, 2009; Sudnow, 1978). Every creative discipline requires the development of concrete knowledge and skills as well as personal exploration. Personal exploration cannot be taught in a concrete manner but a teacher can easily create an environment that encourages that type of discovery learning. *Note: This statement is not meant to impugn the spiritual beliefs of any readers, only to point out that, while some master improvisers demonstrate mysterious sources of inspiration, the pathway to improvisation skill involves personal practice and exploration.*

Improvisation Does Not Require Skill/Technique

Response: Virtuosic improvisation requires that the improviser can technically execute what is in his or her mind's ear. Countless successful improvisers from Jimi Hendrix to John Coltrane have spent endless hours practicing to perfect their improvisation technique. Furthermore, many of the great Western classical composers (Bach, Mozart, Beethoven, Liszt, Chopin) utilized their keen compositional awareness and technique (that is, knowledge of theory and harmony) for improvisation. In fact, to a certain extent, skill limitations open the door for the role of an improvisation teacher. The improvisation teacher can assess a student's skill level and/or potential and frame appropriate activities according to the teacher's evaluation. For example, a student who cannot fluidly perform an E-major scale will probably not be successful improvising over a twelve-bar blues in the key of E. However, that same student might be very successful at improvising over an easier major-scale vamp, such as C major. If the reader wishes to explore this dynamic further, we highly recommend reading Mihaly Csikszentmihalyi's work on "Flow," which addresses the balance between skill and challenge on an individual task (Csikszentmihalyi, 1991).

Improvisation Cannot Be Assessed or Evaluated

Response: With any creative act, there is a certain degree of subjectivity when it comes to evaluating such processes or products. However, creative products have been assessed for centuries. Any assessment of a creative product (improvisation included) will involve a subjective dance between the respective preferences and values of the teacher and the student. Music teachers with little prior improvisation experience can give invaluable feedback based on their musical education and experience. Most importantly, an improvisation teacher should listen with an open mind and consider where a student improviser is coming from and where he or she could go. To assist these conversations and provide meaningful feedback, teachers and students can reference the rubrics, checklists, and other assessments included in this book. Feedback and assessment tools should always be viewed as a means for improvement.

Improvisation, Particularly Free and Group Improvisation, Is Simply Cacophonous Noise

Response: Gabriela Montero, Brad Mehldau, Lennie Tristano, Keith Jarrett, Bobby McFerrin, Lee Konitz, Paul Wertico, Pat Metheny and many others have all participated in very consonant, pleasant, freely unstructured improvisations, to name just a few examples. Dissonance and "cacophony" are contingent upon setting, mood, and personalities.

Older Students Cannot Improvise Without Extensive Prior Experience

Response: Many impressive improvisers have started successfully at many different ages, some after having played notated music their entire life up to a given point. Master jazz trumpeter Terell Stafford began studying jazz after he had completed two degrees in classical trumpet performance. The world renowned concert violinist, Hilary Hahn, began to explore improvisation with the German pianist Hauschka almost sixteen years into her career.

Improvising to Learned Melodies Will Erode Previous Learning

Response: Ensemble directors may express apprehension that creative ornamentation might endanger the performance of concert repertoire. However, alongside the previous point, the authors have taught students to ornament common melodies ("Happy Birthday," "Twinkle, Twinkle, Little Star") for years and not a single student has ever forgotten the original melody. In fact, we have found that such an approach actually strengthens understanding of the original melody, as students must know the structure of the original melody before they can know how to change the melody. Bass virtuoso Rufus Reid discussed this concept in the context of his time as a sideman with saxophone legend Joe Henderson. In particular, Reid (Berliner, 1994) notes that, after thirty years of playing the same "standards," the melodies were "like Silly Putty in his hands," to the point where he could easily quote, transpose, ornament, and weave in and out of a melody at will (p. 226). It should be emphasized that the authors wholeheartedly endorse thorough learning of the original melody before moving on to ornamentation.

Years of "Proper" Technique and Repertoire Must Be Learned Prior to Attempting Improvisation

Response: This myth is particularly unfortunate because some individuals actively discourage improvisation among music students on the basis of this claim. From a purely historical and an anecdotal perspective, the claim seems immediately flawed. Even if we discard the historical records that cite Bach, Mozart, Beethoven, Chopin, and Liszt as brilliant improvisers, composers, and repertoire performers, there are also many contemporary individuals who have pursued parallel studies in both concert repertoire and improvised music. A cursory list of these individuals would include Wynton Marsalis, Robert Levin, Zakir Hussain, Bobby McFerrin, Nina Simone, Herbie Hancock, Eddie Daniels, Gabriela Montero, Bill Evans, Paquito D'Rivera, Uri Caine, Sara Caswell, Keith Jarrett, Bela Fleck, Matt Turner, and Edgar Meyer, to name just a few. There is little historical or scientific evidence that the brain and body cannot develop simultaneous skill in two or more different mediums or styles (history probably would not have experienced the age of the Renaissance if that was the case).

If You Are Not an Experienced Improviser, You Cannot Teach Improvisation

Response: At professional development seminars, conferences, and faculty meetings, music teachers have frequently expressed this concern to us. One could argue that the concern is actually tied up in nuanced awareness of a music genre more than the phenomenon of music improvisation. There is no person who cannot improvise. If we dig more deeply, the real translation for "I cannot improvise" might be "I do not have much experience with jazz harmony." It is important to remember that, while jazz music features a rich history of musical improvisation, jazz music (or any genre) does not encapsulate all improvisation. A lack of jazz knowledge or experience does not mean that a music teacher cannot find an entry point into improvisation. In fact, it is likely that the teacher's musical experience and expertise provide the perfect building blocks for an improvisation activity framed in a certain way. These same building blocks allow the music teacher, regardless of genre expertise, to engage in these experiences.

Researchers have documented teachers' apprehension toward teaching improvisation (Bernhard, 2013; Bernhard & Stringham, 2016; Schopp, 2006). Many dedicated teachers are understandably afraid that they will not adequately serve their students in this area, that they might teach students "wrong things." Teachers need not stress specific genres or areas where they may lack expertise. Instead, we encourage them to trust in their musical and pedagogical skills and listen to emergent musical moments with open ears. Teachers should not let fear hold them back from the level of musical awareness teachers and students will experience by exploring melody, harmony, rhythm, texture, timbre, articulation, and dynamics through the improvisational experiences in this book. Teachers can also help students overcome their own anxieties about improvising by demonstrating a continued commitment to improvisation in the curriculum. As teachers engage in these exercises, they can have an open dialogue about their own apprehensions for activities. In fact, a teacher can be frank and honest and let students know that there will be times that a musical idea will fall flat on its face. Those moments are opportunities to reflect, reset, and refine. The most important thing is that both the teacher and the students are on a larger musical journey that will help all members in the ensemble to listen and create in ways that lead to new musical understandings and collaborative experiences. It can be deeply gratifying for a student to experience a teacher who is willing to take chances and jump in the deep end with them. Teachers should engage in risk taking and exploration alongside the student and simultaneously appreciate the personal contributions and reactions of each student. As Martin Buber (1957) writes, teaching presents a situation "that has never been before and will never come again . . . It demands presence, responsibility; it demands you" (p. 114).

In Section II, we move past the myths that might be holding you back as a music educator from teaching improvisation in your classroom. We prepare your approach to teaching by discussing improvisational teaching and responsive planning. You will learn how to frame your teaching with practical tips for designing and responding to students' improvisation activities. In Section III, we provide thirty-six improvisation lessons for a variety of large ensembles and classroom settings; these lessons are divided into the areas of melody, harmony, rhythm, texture and timbre, articulation, and dynamics. Section IV closes with classroom vignettes that bring the lessons to reality.

Understanding Improvisational Teaching and Responsive Planning

Introduction

In this section, we focus on the teacher as an active facilitator of musical improvisation, in which improvisational teaching and responsive planning combine to create meaningful experiences for students. At first, a discussion on improvisation and planning in teaching may seem rather incongruent: after all, one is spontaneous, while the other is premeditated and structured. But we have found that it is the tension between spontaneity and premeditated planning that enables us to be the most creative and responsive to students' musical needs. Sawyer (2004) explains it best:

> When we realize that creative teaching is improvisational, we see that teachers are creative professionals, requiring not only pedagogical content knowledge but also creative performance skills—the ability to effectively facilitate a group improvisation with students. (p. 17)

As Sawyer suggests, teachers play a vital role in the facilitation of improvisation experiences. It takes teachers' knowledge of pedagogy and content as well as an ability to respond in the moment to creative improvisational experiences to foster musical growth. While this task may at first seem daunting, creative teaching is based on an important principle present in all teaching: listen to and understand students first. If teachers embrace this approach, we believe it can transform their practice into a *responsive pedagogy*. Responsive pedagogy involves the practice of closely monitoring students' past and emergent understandings of music-making, and adapting to students' musical understandings on all levels of music interaction. In doing so, teachers notice and respond to the "substance of student thinking, as it unfolds in class" (Hammer, Goldberg, & Fargason, 2012, p. 4).

Understanding Your Students

A student's musical understandings can best be depicted by Figure 2.1. There are three levels of musical understanding demonstrated in improvisation activities, and these understandings are nested within one another.

First, the student arrives with his or her own cultural understandings of music. We broadly label this as students' *cultural music understandings.* For example, students may think of music in terms of their marching band, beat-making, coffeehouse, worship, or family experiences. Their musical experiences are closely tied to the cultures that they live within. Each setting where music occurs also has certain expectations, such as playing prepared music, using technology, playing by ear, or using certain tonalities while avoiding others. Here are some questions teachers could ask students to have a better sense of their overarching understandings of music:

- What types of music do you listen to in your free time?
- Where do you listen to music in your free time?
- Do you perform music with other people outside of music class? If so, what is the setting like? Do you read music or play by ear?
- What type of music do you play outside of music class?
- What would you like me to know about your musical background and interests?

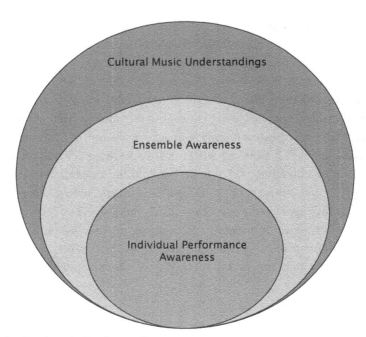

FIGURE 2.1 Students' musical understandings

Kim

Catching Students' Creative Energy

Many teachers wonder when and if their students are ready for more free musical activities. Some can't imagine where it might fit in their school day, or for whom it might work. For that, I encourage teachers to slow down, breathe, and consider these famous words from children's author Norton Juster (1961): "there is much worth noticing that often escapes the eye" (p. 132). I encourage you to look at the in-between moments; students passing in the hallway, standing at the bus stop, gabbing in your room, even their incessant playing while you're trying to talk! What are they talking about? What are they listening to? What rhythms or melodies are they riffing on?

This very thing happened to me in my first year of teaching. I opened up my middle school classroom during lunch for students to practice. While I sat in the corner and munched away on my brown bag lunch and caught up on email, all sorts of chaotic noise enveloped my room. Often I just had to tune it out, but then I couldn't help being drawn into their practice habits.

At first, I paid attention to whether they were practicing how I had asked: first identifying small chunks of challenging sections, playing slowly, and then increasing their speed. But then I started to notice what they did not do, and what they added to the process. They talked with one another quite a bit, they asked each other to listen to one another, and then they added parts to the pieces that we were learning in class. On many occasions one friend would call another friend over and say, "Hey, did you hear how I changed that measure!" or "Do you want to create another version of this tune sort of like [insert biggest pop song]?" They would then sit and improvise possibilities.

I was floored!! No one had prepared me for students with such creative tangents. On top of that, I was not leaving any room for that type of creativity in my classroom. That was the beginning of my listening and noticing the creative energy of my students. It began to change my teaching. That first year I took one small step . . . I listened to them and responded. We took the creative ideas developed in that lunch hour and brought them back to orchestra rehearsals, playing variations on melodies, and asking teachers and principals to listen to what the students had created. It changed the energy in my ensemble, and it changed me.

First, by knowing students' cultural music understandings, teachers can select and plan improvisation activities that support students' successes while also providing incremental performance opportunities that stretch their comfort zones. Teachers will be better prepared to hear and respond to students' spontaneous musical expressions when they have a better sense of their musical backgrounds. Second, as students improvise with others, they demonstrate an understanding of the music happening all around them. We broadly label this response as *ensemble awareness*. At this level, teachers need to monitor students' emerging ability to respond to what other students may be doing around them. While listening, teachers can ask themselves the following types of questions about individuals:

- Does the student hear and respond to a neighbor?
- Does the student hear and respond to something happening on the other side of the ensemble?
- Does the student contribute to the overall form or feeling of the improvisation?
- Does the student take a leadership or accompaniment role in the development of the improvisation?

Finally, the student also demonstrates her own understanding of the music that she is developing in the moment. We define this level as *individual performance awareness*. Teachers play a vital role in observing whether students can develop an improvisation in a cohesive way, and describe their actions. While listening, teachers can ask themselves the following:

- Does the student develop the improvisation in a logical manner?
- Does the student bring back ideas that were used earlier in the improvisation?
- Does a student's improvisations change over time to demonstrate his developing musical understandings?

In discussion, teachers can ask students the following:

- What did you accomplish in your performance?
- Can you describe what you did with your musical ideas? Or, can you remember any of your musical ideas?

As we have engaged students in improvisation activities we have become aware that we must constantly monitor all levels of musical understanding. In one particular group, we had students with backgrounds in jazz, psychedelic rock, folk, Middle Eastern music, marching band, and alternative-rock music. It took some time and interest on our part to familiarize ourselves with these styles.

In that same group, we taught a student from Qatar and she consistently brought her cultural conceptualizations of texture/timbre, melody, harmony, dynamics, and articulation to group improvisation experiences. Her improvisations were also couched in her emerging understanding of the musical form that was being developed in her improvisation groups. We watched her navigate these experiences and respond to others. And finally, on a moment-to-moment basis, we had to watch her respond to each note of her own playing. Could she anticipate how to close a phrase? Could she find a unique idea and develop it? These are the types of questions we asked ourselves as we carefully crafted our responses to her playing.

Kim

Engaging With the Fish Bowl

Have you ever watched how children look at a fish bowl? They stare in wonder, they mimic the fish with pulsing lips, they tap on the glass, and then they wiggle their fingers in the water in hopes that the fish will come up for one kiss. At times, they plunge their hands in the water to try to grab a fish or touch the underwater castle situated at the bottom of the bowl.

I think this is how I *finally am* with improvisatory musical styles and genres. You see, for much of my adult life I have just stared in on interesting musical ideas or practices, admiring them from afar but never thinking they were for me. But I have finally engaged with the fish bowl and am willing to engage over and over again. Like a child, I've mimicked contemporary string performance techniques, I've spoken to string improvisers, sharing my admiration of their performance techniques and asking their opinions, and at times I dived in swimming a bit on the surface to get a broad sense of the style before diving deeply. I still do not feel like an expert and I may not ever feel this way, given the circumstances of my life, but I continue to try to learn and make myself swim. For me it is the waters of Middle Eastern taqsim and Scottish fiddle music that draw me in.

For teachers, problems arise when we think we have to be the fish. We have to swim in the water of that musical style with the same mastery, or we feel we need to label ourselves as a certain kind of fish—an Irish fiddler, a bluegrass player, an alternative-rock player, a Middle Eastern oud expert, and so on. Instead, we need to be willing to engage in that experience, to dive in and explore that environment. Our students need to see us stepping out of our comfort zone, engaging with other musical worlds, and not necessarily expertly swimming in them. We bring those perspectives and questions back to our students, and in doing so, foster a willingness in them to find their fish bowls.

For you as a teacher, it is important to know your students' musical and cultural backgrounds. Once teachers have that foundational understanding, they can closely watch students respond to group developments within an improvisation and the moment-to-moment changes that students are feeling within their own improvisations. With close monitoring on all levels of musical understanding, the teacher is able to understand and respond to the source of a student's improvisation.

Improvisational Teaching Within Lessons

Often times, problems in the large ensemble setting are addressed through direct instruction, particularly when students need clarification and explanation of specific skills. However, such instruction, while appropriate at select times, can be limiting in a group improvisation setting for a number of reasons, including the following:

- The student or students may not be aware of the specific nature of their musical problems.
- The student or students may not be sure of their musical goals within the group.
- The student or students may have different musical goals from those of other members of the group.

To flexibly teach to group improvisation scenarios, a nuanced understanding of one's students and a variety of communicative exchanges is critical. Understanding students and responding to them effectively takes a different type of teaching, one that is not direct, but situated in the moment just as improvisation is itself. The teacher can conceive of improvisational teaching with the following steps:

- Initiate
- Listen
- Discuss
- Adapt

Initiate. Activities will be driven by different goals for students' musical development. For instance, a teacher may have a goal to improve group communication, or broaden students' sense of harmony. As teachers introduce activities, they need to keep in mind that each goal will require different levels of verbal instruction. At times it may be beneficial to be very clear about your teaching goals, and at other times it may be more beneficial for the students to explore musical concepts through the activity and come to a conclusion about what was accomplished through the improvisation. Most importantly, once the activity has been initiated, the teacher should not try to micromanage or handle the improvisation for the students.

Listen. Listening happens in music-making for both the teacher and students. All the students should collaborate in their listening experiences, paying close attention to their own and others' performances, as the improvisation unfolds. The teacher has an even more heightened responsibility to pay attention to students' levels of musical understanding as students spontaneously respond to one another.

Dan

Spontaneous Listening and Responding

The writer Fran Lebowitz (1981) once said, "the opposite of talking isn't listening, the opposite of talking is waiting" (p. 7). Clearly, she is referring to individuals who are waiting for the other person to finish talking so that they can say what is on their minds. This can sometimes be a difficult habit to break. Even if the conversationalist is not "selfish" per se, sometimes the other speaker says something that suddenly makes you think of an experience and you can barely contain your enthusiasm. Other times, without your realizing it, your ego sidles itself into the situation and you want to demonstrate to the other speaker that you have experienced something akin to the given topic.

This conversational issue illustrates one of the components that make group improvisation so difficult. It takes quite a bit of preparation and work to become a master improviser, but then when you are on stage, it can be very difficult to simply wait, listen, and respond to other musicians' contributions. As in our conversation analogy, sometimes our enthusiasm to "demonstrate" what we practiced just takes over. With one class, our students had the most trouble with their open (not based on any predetermined "tune" or "idea") group improvisations with the entire class. For a week or two, Kim and I were not even sure how to diagnose the problem or give recommendations. Then, one day, it occurred to us that all 20 students were playing almost the entire time. Take a moment and imagine 20 people talking at the exact same time . . . it would not make for great conversation, would it? Does this mean that 20 people can never engage in a conversation? Of course not. Picture large meetings, town hall events, focus groups, and so on. These are all different meeting formats but they all have one thing in common (we hope); an ebb and flow of people listening and talking. To go back to the free improvisation class, once we had recommended that the students put their instruments down and listen more, the group improvisations developed much more clarity and direction.

Discuss. Discussion is most often initiated by the teacher after a group improvisation is done. In time, a teacher will often find that students can initiate their own reflection on their performances. It may behoove the teacher to begin with more open-ended questions. Ankney (2014) found that master jazz teachers often initiate discussion with three types of questions: *awareness, comfort,* and *knowledge* questions. Awareness questions can be as simple as "What did you notice? What did you hear?" Or, more specific questions such as "What did you play at the beginning of the improvisation?" Comfort questions get at students' confidence with improvisation: "How did that feel? Did you feel secure?" And knowledge questions are the most specific: "What technique were you using to respond to the trumpet line? What was your source of influence in that solo?" Questioning also depends on goals. If the teacher's goal was collaboration, she might ask, "Did that feel cohesive?" If a teacher remains open ended with the initial questioning, students are more likely to reveal their broad musical understandings. Students may hear something that was not the main goal of the lesson, or they may share a certain insecurity.

All of these answers should be revealing to the teacher for the choice of future improvisation activities. Remember, as a teacher you can always get more specific later. It is far more difficult to start with specific questions. If a teacher starts with specific questions, students are more likely to respond to teacher questions and discard some of their other spontaneous emergent musical understandings.

Adapt. The final stage of improvisational teaching is to adapt to students' musical understandings and carefully realign goals. This process is different from thinking about a performance in terms of a final product. Instead, a teacher adapts practice to allow students to process musical information in a way that extends their thinking on a musical element. We experienced this in one scenario as we taught students improvisations grounded in certain meters. We thought they were ready to keep track of their place in certain meters, but they were not. They got lost in feeling two or four bars of rests. We realized we had to come back to basic understandings of time and meter (See Section III: Lessons—Rhythm). Once these basics had been established, we encouraged them to work around time in certain meters. Their concept of groove and time expanded widely and we were able to move into sophisticated metrical shifts present in Hindustani raga. This realignment in our planning took a huge "pause" and "reset" on our part as educators. We are trained as educators to stay the course, so adopting an adaptive mindset can take time, but even mild adaptations to activities can reap major musical benefits for students.

Improvisational Teaching Across Lessons

All musical activities are in some way a balance between process and product. The concert pianist practices and rehearses for a scheduled recital. The composer finishes a chamber work so that parts can be distributed to all the musicians for performance. The recording engineer finalizes the balance for a band's new demo. Improvisation, to be sure, also has its products in the form of performances and recordings. However, as we have previously illustrated, the improviser cannot *reproduce* a performance. Thus, there is an especially acute focus on *process* for musical improvisation. It behooves the music teacher to embrace this focus on process not only in a musical sense but in a pedagogical sense as well. To do so requires continual evaluation and instantaneous response, resulting in a musical expression that reflects the performer's organic and unfiltered musical understanding. We find that inviting students to hear these spontaneous musical expressions as a process rather than a product helps everyone adapt or tweak his or her music-making in future improvisation experiences.

When a teacher continually incorporates the improvisational activities in this book, or activities inspired by lessons in this book, he can move on to thinking about improvisational teaching across lessons. Figure 2.2 captures improvisational teaching across lessons during a 10-week academic quarter in a free improvisation class. The reader can feel free to adapt the broad ideas from the figure for her own academic calendar and schedule. As teachers, we frequently opt to record every two weeks. Students are recorded while

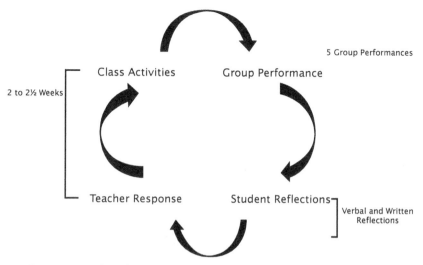

FIGURE 2.2 Improvisational teaching across lessons

they are performing an open-ended free group improvisation, for a total of five record-ings. These performances are unprompted by ideas from the teacher or students. The goal is to simply spontaneously collaborate and make music together. These recorded per-formances are particularly important for reflection, which happens through verbal and written formats. Students are invited to comment after the performance on what they felt or heard, and they can be assigned to go home and review the recording on SoundCloud or other web-based applications and write a reflection. The teacher should frame future improvisation experiences around students' feedback. We suggest that teachers verbally respond to what was heard in the performances, and when possible, respond to students' written reflections.

Improvisational teaching across lessons can also be flexibly adopted in the tradi-tional school ensemble. The time given to improvisation activities may not be as extensive per class, but the elements of group performance, student reflection, teacher response, and class activity re-planning can and should always be present. A band teacher could include two 15-minute improvisation activities a week over the entire school year. While this time allotment may at first feel odd to students, they will eventually come to expect these improvisation experiences during class and enjoy them as changes from the struc-ture of ensemble rehearsals. The band teacher can look closely at the group's literature to determine what musical elements need refinement and then bring students together to explore these concepts through their improvisations. Free group improvisation perform-ances could be recorded every five improvisation lessons and students could listen and reflect on them online. In rehearsal, students could use these autonomous experiences to reflect more critically on their own performances. And finally, hearing a teacher's re-sponse to improvisations would be important in order for students to understand the direction of upcoming improvisation activities.

Kim

Tag! You're It!

Recently, I was watching my preservice students guide free improvisation activities and I became increasingly aware of the dance they were doing as they sequenced their instructions and asked questions in real time. It felt like a game of tag, and it reminded me of how I felt when I began teaching this way, or how I still feel when I am trying a new activity.

When you are working with large groups of students all looking to you for direction and inspiration (with no music in front of them to read), it can be a bit intimidating. During their peer teachings, my students quickly burst into a game of "tag," giving directives such as "imitate this painting," "pass this rhythm around until it changes," or "move stepwise until you harmonize with a neighbor." Their peers were "it" and would hastily respond to whatever musical directive was given by creating something, anything, so that the musical runaround could quickly be passed off for a teacher response. You see, in this game of tag both the students and the teacher were uncomfortable.

I believe much of the discomfort from this frenetic game can be assuaged with a bit of framing by the teacher. We can contextualize what is about to happen in an activity, or what has just happened. We have to help students zoom out and think of the whole in an improvisation activity, rather than think of it as a series of moves that are passed off from one person to the next. For instance, in the "Deep Listening Dynamics" activity described in Section III, it may be that students successfully send dynamics across the ensemble and changes occur student to student. However, if students cannot envision what the ensemble sounds like as a whole, much of the activity is lost. When a teacher is tagged for a response, he should not only be willing to challenge more students to pass the dynamics across the ensemble but he should also help the students pause and reflect on what is being heard as a whole, perhaps asking, "If our piece was a 3D image, what would it look like from the audience?" Students might respond by saying it was like a shifting city with buildings growing in size and then shrinking again. This reaction would give way to a sense of what is needed on the ensemble level, and suddenly the "every man for himself" game of tag would move to a group conversation.

Setting this tone is important. From the beginning, teachers should let students know that there will be room to reflect on their improvisations through discussion or writing (see Section II: "The Center of Improvisational Teaching: Assessing Growth"). One improvisation experience is not the end of what the students will feel and change in their performances of melody, harmony, rhythm, texture/timbre, articulation and/or dynamics. Instead they can come back to these musical elements, playing with them not only in group improvisations but also in their own personal practices and, if applicable, in ensemble rehearsals. Improvisation is simply the beginning of an ongoing journey of refining musicianship and personal expression. Finding time to respond to students' improvisations may seem like a stretch to a large ensemble teacher. We recommend being realistic about what teachers and students can accomplish together. Teachers can start simply with verbal feedback by using some of the questioning techniques described previously. If students work in small groups and create recordings, a teacher could listen to these recordings on the go and be able to give feedback to the small group through an online format. For instance, teacher comments for a large band of 60 students could be streamlined into 12 group comments. Receiving teacher feedback[1] every three weeks on their development would assure students of their efforts and send a message to them that their musical understandings matter.

1. For an additional resource on assessment practices in large ensembles see Duke, R. A. (2005). *Intelligent music teaching: Essays on the core principles of effective instruction.* Austin, TX: Learning and Behavior Resources.

The Center of Improvisational Teaching: Assessing Growth

Assessing student growth in improvisation can seem like a particularly challenging task when one considers how an improvised performance that was once there is then quickly gone. However, assessment is really at the heart of all improvisational teaching. Teachers have to closely hear, see, respond, and initiate meaningful activities that change or extend the educational experience for students. Assessment is mutually beneficial to both the student and the teacher when it is part of a continuum of relational experiences that help both parties improve the learning environment. There is a vast array of performance skills and reflective thinking that go into improvisation performances that can be thoughtfully captured and noted through a variety of assessment strategies.

Flexibility in Assessing Growth

Elliot Eisner (2002) explains that a teacher can "measure without evaluating, evaluate without testing, and assess without grading ... evaluating need not focus only on the product of a student's work; it can focus on the process as well" (p. 189). In this book, we focus less on the improvised performance as the product and turn toward examining the process of improvisation as it reflects musical learning and growth. For these goals, teachers can collect evidence of student learning through a variety of formats, including live or recorded performance, verbal discussion and written reflection on performance, and also reflection on the cumulative skills and knowledge that lead toward improvisation. This archival information provides a story of a student's journey with musical elements such as melody, harmony, rhythm, texture/timbre, articulation, and dynamics. Or as Eisner explains,

> The teacher might aim to evaluate how the student engaged in his or her
> work ... the student's willingness to take risks ... the manner in which a student
> goes about his or her work, the ways in which problems are solved, his or her

willingness to ask questions or to speculate about possibilities. There is a host of qualities displayed in the processes the student employs that can say much to teachers about how the student works. (Eisner, 2002, p. 181)

As teachers embark on observing students' work in improvisation, they have to think of their role in reflecting on students' musical thought processes. The first step is to back away from solely observing and commenting on overall ensemble sound. But if a teacher embraces improvisational teaching by initiating, listening, discussing, and adapting practice to students' levels of music understanding, then a teacher is more able to collect archival tidbits of individual student knowledge throughout improvisation activities.

Informally, teachers are memory keepers of learning experiences that play out on a daily basis in their classrooms. They notice student progress through performance and discussion and can make mental notes of student growth through these experiences. This approach is very important for developing a responsive pedagogy, but equally important is finding ways to document individual student growth and adapting practices through assessment strategies. As they decide on adaptations for future lessons, teachers should make note of discussions and comments after students' improvised performances, and students should provide reflection on performance in other ways that allow teachers to more carefully document individual student growth. In several of the assessment strategies, we suggest that students reflect on their performances through written activities, journals, or blogs. In this way, a teacher can document individual awareness of their listening and performance knowledge, their understanding of group dynamics, and how they adapted their playing in real time (see Figure 2.1).

Rather than conceiving of improvisation activities in terms of prescriptive assessments, Eisner (2002) suggests that arts assessments might be better thought of as a responsive evaluation of student performance, based on expressive outcomes. "Expressive outcomes are the outcomes that students realize in the course of a curriculum activity, whether or not they are the particular outcomes sought" (p. 161). For example, in the lesson *Pedal to the Metal* (see Section III: Lessons—Harmony) students may discover that dissonance can actually be instructive. More specifically, by freely "trying out" different note combinations, students can inductively explore the relationships of different musical intervals instead of abstractly reading about them in a textbook. In fact, sitting on dissonant tones and finding ways out of them can be quite pleasing to the ear. Instruction can thrive when teachers are open to hearing what students have experienced in the course of improvisation activities and begin their evaluations through more open-ended prompts. In doing so, teachers are more open to hearing students' broad musical understandings even if they do not align with larger lesson goals. As teachers are open to hearing and responding to students they take on a stance of responsive evaluation, which Robert Stake (1973) defined as being reliant on "natural communication" and in doing so, follow their natural tendencies to "observe and react" to whatever the situation entails (p. 11).

Embracing Students' Musical Journeys

As frustrating as it might seem to some, teachers who seek a concrete, "prescriptive" approach to teaching group improvisation might find such an approach to be elusive. At its heart, improvisation first fosters *divergent thinking* (thinking that does not have a clear-cut right/wrong answer, but generates many possible solutions) as a creative activity and, second, it is a musical journey toward the student finding his musical personality. The choices that students make in the arts reflexively demonstrate their unique musical understandings and aesthetic preferences. The inherent challenge in assessing a student improvisation is the balance between the music teacher's expert knowledge of best skills and practices with the student's situation-specific spontaneous performance. The immediacy and inability to preplan improvisation presents opportunities for students to react to a unique musical moment with these understandings and dispositions; we refer to this ability to react as the student's "spontaneous self." Spolin (1999) describes the feeling that is the result of experiencing the *spontaneous self*, suggesting that "through spontaneity we are re-formed into ourselves. It creates an explosion that for the moment frees us from handed-down frames of reference, memory choked with old facts and information and undigested theories and techniques of other people's findings" (p. 4).

As students are on a road to personal discovery with their musicianship through improvisation, teachers need to keep the students' unique voices in mind. Think, for a moment, about your unique speaking style. It is likely that a close friend can realize that it is you after one sentence of conversation. You have a particular voice timbre, a particular enunciation, a particular vocabulary, and so on. If you tried to speak like somebody else for a day (or even an hour) you would probably become either exhausted or annoyed by the sheer effort of sustaining such a contrived, unnatural approach. Creative music works in a similar manner. A more linear approach to phrasing might be natural to one person, while a more angular approach may be more natural to another.

A tight rhythmic feel might be more natural to one person, while a looser rhythmic feel might be more natural to another. As teachers watch the development of individuals' musicianship they may ask themselves the following: How have students' musical voices changed over time? How have they used their musical voices to complement or extend musical activities? And have they found other musicians to work with to extend their musical voices? As students work to improvise within particular styles or with certain techniques, the questions can become more focused within the genre: Have they found rhythmic grooves that fit the style yet are their own? Have they mastered when to use certain timbres appropriately but applied uniquely to enhance the overall feel of the music? Or have they been able to create extended solos that blend their ideas well with techniques covered in class?

Responding to Students' Experiences

When music teachers aim to see the individual and make note of her growth, they are better prepared to respond to student learning in meaningful ways. Responding to students' experiences is where assessment really comes into play; students gain a sense of how teachers and peers view their progress in their musical journey. To make improvisation assessment meaningful and complete, *immediate* feedback can be crucial. No one likes feeling judged, particularly during improvisation. Instead if all the students in the classroom embrace improvisation as a space to voice their unique musical selves, then feedback is framed accordingly and can help develop each young musician. Furthermore, teachers need to emphasize a rather humbling fact to students: Failure in improvisation is an absolute necessity in the learning process. Failure should not only be expected, but it should also be encouraged.

The instructor experiences a subjective dilemma with any artistic or personal endeavor, whether it is creative writing, studio art, or an improvisation class: The assessment of a divergent activity rarely involves binary right/wrong scenarios but instead is based on professional judgments developed through expertise. The professional knowledge and "gut" instinct of an experienced musician often informs the instructor when something is not working. Of course, instincts are commonly equated with subjective opinions but there are also cultural norms that inform this "gut" instinct. A very common example involves jazz improvisation. If a student plays behind the tempo, it will sound "wrong" or like "dragging" to an experienced musician. There is nothing wrong with pointing this problem out to a student but there is a case to be made that the *approach* to feedback is critical. For example, if a jazz instructor says, "Dan, you're dragging," this is *problem-identifying feedback*. Although we must *identify* the problem before we can *solve* it, this approach does not really leave me with a productive path forward unless I am either an existing jazz expert or an unusually motivated student. If the teacher embraces the full dimensionality of the "problem," she can give full *problem-solving feedback*. The teacher may notice that the student's phrases are crowded with notes and that is why he is having trouble staying in time. Instead of saying, "Dan, you're dragging," the teacher can take more of a problem-solving approach by saying, "Dan, I noticed you're playing a ton of notes, and not leaving much space, and it is making it very difficult for you to play in time. Why don't you explore some shorter phrases that you like with more space in between?"

Dan

Practicing Spontaneity?

One of the toughest aspects of improvisation is the ability to balance knowledge and skill with the ability to be loose and embrace spontaneity. I myself have always struggled with the latter part. Growing up near the New York City jazz scene, I watched brilliant jazz musicians practice and study endlessly and then seemingly flip a switch in their brain that turned their "thinking" part off and their "imaginative" part on.

This concept actually applies to any activity that features spontaneous emergence. Whether it is playing basketball, leading a meeting, or teaching a class, these individuals need to be able to turn their brains away from a scripted, preplanned procedure. Charlie Parker famously said, "You've got to learn your instrument. Then, you practice, practice, practice. And then, when you finally get up there on the bandstand, forget all that and just wail" (Pugatch, 2006, p. 73). Mastering one's instrument is certainly no easy task but I think people like me are drawn more to that part because it is made up of reasonably clear sequential goals. Whereas, when it is time to perform (or play basketball or speak in public without a script), you are essentially functioning with a blank slate and reinventing yourself with each new set of emergent events. As scholar/improviser Ed Sarath (1996) has noted, going into such a situation with a script in mind essentially blocks your mind to all of the wonderful emergent possibilities that are presented to you on a second-to-second basis.

You can practice a lot of things as an improviser but you can never *practice* all of the second-to-second occurrences that one cannot anticipate. From my perspective, I have found that I need to give myself and my students permission to follow their whims and react to what they hear. It can be amazingly difficult for students to do this. Much of their life habits have been conditioned to follow specific instructions. Fortunately, if the teacher keeps throwing musical curveballs at the students, encourages active listening and flexibility, and coordinates constructive group reflections on recent improvisations, many students do learn to become more comfortable with spontaneity. Kim and I had this experience with one improvisation class performance. After weeks and weeks of challenging prompts, active listening, and group reflections, the students gave an open-ended group free improvisation performance that seemed to be reaching its natural end, when a cellist suddenly played a countermelody in a new key. Immediately, the rest of the group followed the cellist and improvised beautifully for another five minutes until the improvisation ended. Kim and I could not have been prouder. *This* is the whole point of group music improvisation. The students spontaneously reacted to a momentary musical change and morphed the entire mood of the performance in a way that nobody could have anticipated.

In more open-ended group improvisation, it can be more difficult to identify problems, because of a lack of cultural norm boundaries or a unique mix of different student dynamics. This is where it becomes even more important to engage the students in both the problem-finding and the problem-solving process instead of offering only your own feedback. In particular, the usefulness of responsive pedagogy is that it targets student intentionality. For example, a group improvisation may have sounded muddled but you, as the teacher, are not sure why. A student might tell you or write in a response that he kept trying to execute this idea but it just was not working. This is where the verbal dialogue is particularly helpful. The teacher can ask questions such as the following:

- Why did you *keep* trying if it felt as if it weren't working? Why not move on to something else?
- While you were trying to do this, how hard were you listening to the other members of the group?
- Instead of trying to execute something, why don't you try to accompany some other members of the group and see how that feels?

For instance in another group, the reason for the "muddled" music could have been something completely different. There might have been too many amplified guitars. Everybody might have been trying to play at the same time. There might have been too many players occupying the middle range. The difficulty of assessing improvisation can be much like traveling to a destination. There are always many paths to a destination but we know when we are lost.

While it may take some time to get used to identifying issues and responding with open and flexible questioning, remember that it is far better than offering suggestions in the binary. Teachers should be wary of directive language such as "fix this." This language is rarely useful in improvisation development because rather than encouraging problem-solving, it simply points out a problem.

Knowing that feedback through assessment is helpful for growth and for changing teacher practice, we designed our lessons with both formative and summative assessment suggestions. With formative assessments, grades and final evaluations are pushed to the side and responses to performance come through verbal feedback or through writing or musical demonstrations. In certain lessons we give question prompts, while in others we provide reflection activities for students and groups on their performances. In all of these activities the most important variable is that feedback not be overlooked. Feedback needs to be viewed as central to students' musical development, even if the experience felt like a failure. Remember that failure is a necessary step in long-term improvisation development. It is all about how the "failure" is framed. If the teacher or peer offering feedback frames an issue as a problem to be solved, student improvisers are more likely to explore finding a musical solution.

In contrast, summative assessments are a final evaluation, and often given in the form of a letter grade. We present a selection of rubrics and criteria lists that should be used only for summative evaluation after students have had ample time to explore musical concepts and have used the assessment tool themselves in self- or peer-assessments of formative experiences. In fact, we recommend that teachers and students work together to create assessment tools that meet the goals of the improvisation activity and any other issues that may have arisen from responsive evaluations. In this way, the evaluation of student learning and growth is clear and can be aligned to the growth of musicians within an ensemble or class.

We also suggest a number of summative assessments that evaluate students' corequisite music skills and knowledge for improvisation. For example, students might be asked to play a certain rhythm, to apply a certain harmony, or to listen and comment on great improvisers and improvisation styles. None of these experiences, in and of themselves, constitute improvisation performance. However, together they represent the types of corequisite skills that inform improvisation performance. In such instances, teachers are assessing students' knowledge and skills to support an improvisation experience, not the improvisation performance itself.

Encouraging Flexibility, Responsivity, and Open-Mindedness

To put it in plain terms, some of your students are going to think that improvised music sounds "weird." The problem is common to arts education and is also reflective of larger cultural implications. One is probably not going out on a limb too much by saying that, on the whole, non-improvised music tends to be more popular than improvised music, at least in the United States. Most popular music features little or no improvisation. There is a purported story that, after the horn section players took amazing improvised solos on the first *Blood, Sweat, and Tears* album, the musicians had to transcribe their own solos and memorize them for future concerts. The story goes that, even though the horn section was made up of brilliant improvisers, their audience would expect and desire the same solos from the record.

Debating the philosophy behind the story is beyond the scope of this book, but it is worth noting that many individuals are unnerved by improvised music and many of those individuals will make up a teacher's music class. Anecdotally, many people ascribe their reluctance to listen to improvised music to dissonance, cacophony, randomness, and/or a general lack of discernible musical structure. One can make the case that certain recordings (e.g., Ornette Coleman's double quartet on *Free Jazz*, John Coltrane's ensemble on *Ascension*) and certain cultural stereotypes (fans of the great mockumentary, *This Is Spinal Tap*, always reference the hilarious "free-form jazz odyssey" scene) have given many individuals the perception that all improvisation, particularly free or group improvisation, exhibits these qualities. Bringing the focus back to the music classroom, we think that whether your students are familiar with Ornette Coleman or not (most probably will not be familiar), it is likely that they will be less culturally familiar with improvised music, as opposed to the popular or other music styles they listen to on a regular basis.

Getting Students Past the Giggles

It is critical that, when implementing the lesson plans in Section III, the teacher be acutely aware of both the existing student culture and the extent to which the students must stretch their comfort level for a given lesson plan. Elements of student culture such as age and school environment can contribute to student reception. An enthusiastic elementary school orchestra might eagerly tackle these activities, whereas a high school band with no prior experience in improvisation might erupt in giggles and snickers.

Although the situation will vary from program to program, we make the following recommendations:

1. Some of your students will enjoy improvising immediately, while others will experience paralyzing fear. Neither one of these reactions is "wrong" and all of your students deserve your empathy in this process. The fastest way to permanently turn students off to improvisation is to force them to participate or to criticize their reluctance. Remember, you can always include reluctant students either by having them listen to the activity until they are ready to actively participate or by having them participate as part of a "group" improvisation texture instead of a "solo" texture. Above all, express patience with your students and do not become discouraged. Ed List comments on this perfectly in his *Creative Director* volumes: "You will experience some 'giggling' in the early stages . . . the above are only temporary and will no longer exist after the second rehearsal! Once the basic concepts are introduced, your procedures will continue to unfold and expand relative to your musical expectations" (1991 p. 217).

2. Have a sense of humor. This will sound like a strange statement for this book but . . . *Not all of these activities will be successful* . . . we'll repeat that again: *Not all of these activities will be successful.* It is just as unreasonable to suggest that all improvisations will be appealing as it is to expect that a composer can compose a piece without going back and changing anything. This concept may sound disconcerting but there is good news. Improvisation growth is a long-term process and sometimes the performances that are epic failures are more educational than successful performances. A sense of humor in such instances will teach students to be daring and grow from disappointing improvisations, instead of receding into apprehension.

3. In the face of apprehension, proceed slowly in a piecemeal fashion, if necessary. There is no need to launch into the full extent of a lesson right away. Many of the lessons are broken into components; feel free to have students participate in part of an activity before taking it on in the fullest sense.

4. There is no need to use a full ensemble for every single lesson. In fact, we have found that breaking the larger ensemble into smaller groups of about ten to twelve can be very beneficial for developing listening and responding skills. Feel free to try out these lessons on sectional or lesson groups, if applicable. Do not hesitate to use only a few minutes of your class or rehearsal for one of these lessons. These lessons are intended to streamline into the normal activities of the ensemble/class without interfering with them.

We should note that improvisation does not need to be dissonant, texturally cacophonous, random, or structureless. However, with the unpredictable collaborative emergence that occurs in musical improvisation, some of these qualities are bound to emerge from time to time. Moreover, the patient music teacher should encourage students to experience these elements as part of the learning process. It would certainly be fair to say that these musical elements are found in much of the raw, expressionistic music of Anthony Braxton, Cecil Taylor, and Albert Ayler, but it is important to keep a few things in mind:

1. Improvisation is not automatically dissonant, cacophonous, random, or structureless.
2. All of the musical characteristics just listed are part of a subjective context.

In particular, we stress the first point because there are countless instances of improvisation that sound quite structured and exquisite. Fans rarely describe Keith Jarrett's (1975) *Köln Concert*, Dexter Gordon's (1962) classic solo on "I Guess I'll Hang My Tears Out to Dry," Paco de Lucia's flamenco guitar work, or Gabriella Montero's classically inspired piano improvisations as anything but beautiful. As we have stated before, improvisation has the remarkable ability to define the *spontaneous self*. A student's spontaneous self will not be the same as Cecil Taylor's spontaneous self or anybody else's for that matter. It may be more or less dissonant, more or less structured, but it will not be the same. Improvised music distinguishes itself because it is both unique and spontaneous. Improvised music must be unique; we know so because a musician who claims to be an improviser cannot perform the exact same thing over and over again, just as a composer cannot be taken seriously if he writes the same thing over and over again. Improvised music distinguishes itself in that it must be spontaneous; otherwise it would fall into the same category as composition, in which participants can go back and edit their unique products (Sarath, 1996).

The question becomes how we, as teachers, encourage students to engage in a type of music that may unnerve students because it is not particularly popular or commonly experienced in listening circles. Instead of focusing on whether dissonance is good or bad, we recommend that the teacher focus on the student's discovery of her spontaneous self. Cecil Taylor required a lot of dissonance for the expression of his spontaneous self, but your student is not Cecil Taylor. Your student is a unique version of himself. The question is not whether or not to encourage dissonance or cacophony in your students' improvisations. The question is how those elements figure into a student's spontaneous self. We, as teachers, cannot know the answer to that question in advance. What we *can* do is encourage flexibility, responsivity, and open-mindedness.

Engaging these qualities can be one of the most difficult things to do as a teacher. It is why teaching a course like college-level creative writing is so difficult. It is assumed that the students have learned grammar, syntax, and style, and have read many great authors. But does that background automatically lead to a creative plot, identifiable characters, and emotive undertones? Of course not. Teaching musical improvisation can feel vexing because the teacher can identify useful practices and commonly prescribed skills but the student is coming into contact with her own lifetime of past experiences. This disparity is why many educators refer to "constructivism" as the way that students *construct* their learning experience from prior networks of experience and new information. Fortunately, it is quite possible for a teacher to teach tried-and-true best practices while also encouraging flexibility, responsivity, and open-mindedness.

The teacher can engage student *flexibility* by encouraging students to explore and try out musical ideas. More specifically, they can improvise with other students without the requirements of a strict performance. For decades, rock and jazz musicians have referred to this as "jamming" or playing in "sessions." This is a terrific opportunity for students to try out ideas in a group setting. Students should also be encouraged to pursue ideas on their own. If they are motivated to practice on their own, encourage them to set aside five or ten minutes for exploration and experimentation. Remember, all of this is very personal. What is dissonant to one student may not be dissonant to another. What is unique to one student might be plain weird to another. We like to equate the exploration process with scientific experiments. The public is aware of scientific discoveries but is rarely aware of how many times an experiment had to fail before the scientist landed on the right approach. We live in a culture that fears mistakes. This fear is anathema to improvisation. There is a great quotation (source unknown) that states "a composer's best tool is his eraser." The improviser's version of this quote might be *mistakes are an improviser's best tool because they show her the road to the style she desires.* Or to cite more succinct and memorable quotations from some of history's greatest improvisers (Rowe, 2010),

> "Sometimes you can fix something that went wrong with what you do next and make it better than it would have been if it hadn't gone wrong . . ." —Bela Fleck

> "Sometimes mistakes are the best thing that can happen, because they might lift you . . . out of your complacency, and open your mind up to a whole other area that you wouldn't have gone to intentionally." —Bobby McFerrin

> "If you don't make mistakes, you aren't really trying." —Coleman Hawkins

> "If you hit a wrong note, then make it right by what you play afterwards." —Joe Pass

> "It was when I found out I could make mistakes that I knew I was onto something." —Ornette Coleman

> "It's taken me all my life to learn what not to play." —Dizzy Gillespie

Responsivity can be encouraged by prompting students to listen. One of the great misconceptions surrounding music education is that, if music is performed within earshot of students then that means that they are listening. Active listening, wherein the individual cognitively engages his aural perceptions, takes serious effort. It is difficult to impossible to become a fluent improviser if the student is not an active listener. Moreover, it is very difficult to develop active listening skills if the students are focused on playing or singing all the time, not unlike conversation, when it is very difficult to simultaneously listen while you are talking. In a revealing interview, saxophonist John Zorn discusses the innovative guitarist Bill Frisell. Zorn notes that one of Frisell's outstanding qualities is his willingness to hang in the musical background and simply listen and soak in what is going on in the music. More specifically, Zorn states, "Bill Frisell is the kind of player who sits back and lets everybody else make decisions and just plays his butt off. Ultimately, he was the one that was making the sound of the music while other people were dealing with the structure of it" (Bailey, 1992, p. 78). One of the ways that teachers can encourage responsivity is to block out a little time for active listening. Consider the following examples:

- Have one group of students perform an improvisation while another group listens and comments afterwards.
- Have students participate in a group improvisation but instruct them to play only approximately a third of time. The rest of the time should be used for active listening. Individual students should listen for entry points for responsive and communicative playing.

Dan

Ego

As I have developed more experience teaching music and performing, I have become more acutely aware of ego. In fact, one can make the case that ego is directly related to any serious activity, including improvisation.

For years, I have never considered myself a person who had an "ego problem." When I heard term ego, I imagined athletes who think they are more important than their team, or politicians who were mired in scandal because they thought that they were such a big deal that they would never get caught. These are certainly classic examples of ego but ego is more complex and manifold than that.

My old conception of ego certainly works with music and music improvisation. There are certainly musicians and improvisers who think very highly of themselves. Some of them are great and, unfortunately, some of them are not as great as they think. But there are also less vain or "bigheaded" examples of ego in music. Consider the following examples:

- Playing what you think would sound cool *instead of what you feel.*
- Playing what you think the audience wants to hear *instead of what you feel.*
- Playing what you think is right or appropriate *instead of what you feel.*
- Playing what you think your teacher would approve *instead of what you feel.*

> One of the toughest things about teaching improvisation is learning to encourage your students to play what *they feel* instead of what they think that you want them to play. A wonderful jazz pianist named Michael Kanan notes that great artists say, "I love *you*" with their music, not "Please love *me!*"
>
> Music students constantly slip into playing what was just practiced or what they think the group would enjoy. But how does a music teacher who typically addresses concrete concepts such as pitch and rhythm inspire musical sincerity and honesty? Encourage your students to listen and react. Spontaneous listening is the great conqueror of ego. Such musical sincerity will reveal itself when the student listens and reacts in the moment instead of forcing a strained, preplanned idea. Anthony Davis addresses this phenomenon with one of my favorite quotations: "In order to listen, you don't necessarily follow, you respond. You try to construct something that coexists or works well with something else—not necessarily this tail-wagging-the-dog thing where you follow someone else" (Borgo, 2007, p. 16).

Encouraging *open-mindedness* can also be challenging. For a teacher, it can be easy to get defensive or intellectually superior when somebody dislikes a musical style that you favor or vice versa. Remember that *this attitude is not open-mindedness.* Open-mindedness is more about dialogue and trying new experiences. Real dialogue can feel like strange terrain for music teachers because we are understandably charged to maintain order through classroom management. The teacher might play one of the recommended recordings from this book for her students and one of the students might say, "That's weird." The teacher's first instinct might be to interpret that statement as an indicator of insolence (it may or may not be; it depends on the behavioral motivation) and become defensive. But maybe the student is not saying this purely for attention; perhaps he really does not understand why people value this music. A more advisable response would be to dig more deeply with more questions. Ask your student why he thinks the music sounds weird and how he might get his own improvisations to sound different. Ask the student about his favorite musicians. Although improvisational music is not "broadly" popular, improvisational music can incorporate the elements of different musical styles (see Section III: Lessons—Rhythm, particularly "Rhythmic Mash-Up" and "Techno Music"). Another recommended response would be to validate the student's comment and encourage flexibility, listening, and open-mindedness. An example is a comment such as "that's totally fine; nobody is saying that you have to enjoy this recording. The purpose of this exercise is not for you to replicate the recording; the purpose is for you to improvise music that you like. The recordings are there to give you some samples and ideas." The student probably will not turn around and say, "Gee whiz, I had this all wrong," but the important thing is that the teacher is making the student engage his value perceptions and dig more deeply into the music specifics. Sometimes students can take baby steps in less comfortable musical situations as they slowly familiarize and develop awareness. The worst thing that a teacher can do is to project an attitude of intellectual superiority. When a teacher gets defensive of her preferences or musical examples, it is not uncommon for a student to immediately shut down. Any further hope of engaging that student in the unfamiliar music is gone.

Constantly reinforce that each student's musical spontaneous self is unique and valid. Is this view meant to reference the "everything is good and everybody gets a trophy philosophy?" No, there is still the element of performance *execution*. Furthermore, anybody who has good self-esteem can probably tell you that trophies have little to do with the real appreciation of self. As Berliner (1994) notes in his magnificent ethnography of master jazz improvisers, these masters spent their lifetimes figuring out their fundamental musical vocabulary and a means of technically executing that vocabulary. After all, if we could all snap our fingers and sing like Bobby McFerrin or play like Bela Fleck, we probably would. But that is not the way that it works; those musicians have spent decades practicing their discipline and developing their spontaneous selves so that they can consistently execute improvisational greatness on the stage. Fortunately, at least according to this book, the sole purpose of arts education is *not* to create virtuoso artists but to engage students in enriching and enjoyable artistic experiences. We encourage teachers to provide constructive feedback while *also* validating students' spontaneous selves. An example of such a statement could be "you demonstrated some really interesting linear contours in your solo but you were sort of stuck in the key of C major. Let's practice playing those contours in some other keys because I think you're really onto something; we just need to expand your palette."

Organization of Lessons

This book takes a streamlined approach to improvisation instruction that is focused on the knowledge and skill development of six broad musical areas:

1. Melody
2. Harmony
3. Rhythm
4. Texture and timbre
5. Articulation
6. Dynamics

The lessons are intended to serve as improvisatory learning vehicles for basic music knowledge and skills. The desired benefit is the development of musical skills through improvisation that are simultaneously requisite to performing repertoire. The hope is that an improvisation activity in the "Articulation" unit may strengthen students' performance and understanding of articulations in all areas of their performance. More specifically, some of these activities work well as pre-repertoire warm-ups and others are structured to specifically enhance repertoire performance. This book also takes a more *process-centered* approach to lessons and activities. Although some of these activities provide good performance/product opportunities, the gist of this book is on flexible process-based activities. As such, they allow the teacher to choose to spend, for instance, two minutes or one hour on a given activity. Furthermore, these lessons are not tied to a particular type of activity. Many of these lessons can be used as a warm-up, a performance work, or simply as a fun stand-alone activity.

Lessons for a Variety of Large Ensemble and Class Settings

The book includes lessons for jazz ensemble, instrumental/choral ensembles, and improvisation ensembles at the beginning and intermediate levels with some extensions for advanced ensembles. While the lessons are flexible and adaptable across ensembles, lessons have been designated for certain groups because the instrumentation or style may fit certain groups better than others. However, teachers are encouraged to use the resources in ways that best suit their teaching situation.

Instrumental/Choral Ensembles

Instrumental and/or choral ensemble lessons are meant to address the three most common ensembles in K–12 music programs in the United States: concert band, orchestra, and choir. For the sake of simplicity, these three ensembles were merged into one category. Although these three ensembles feature distinctly different performance approaches, the lesson plans were designed so that the activities could be easily performed by all three ensembles. Concert bands, orchestras, and choirs often face similar performance expectations, and these lessons are approachable and flexible enough to include within the demands of a regular concert schedule.

Jazz Ensembles

During the past several decades of the jazz education movement, a plethora of jazz method books of various forms have emerged in the market. This book is not written to retread the ground of established jazz improvisation pedagogy methods but to simply outline jazz ensemble improvisation activities that may be explored less frequently in K–12 settings. There are many fine resources for topics such as jazz harmony, patterns, etudes, and rhythmic examples. The lessons in this book emphasize process over product and are more exploratory in nature. A few of the activities are loosely influenced by more avant-garde artists such as Ornette Coleman and Sun-Ra. The activities are designed so that they can be used by both big bands or small group combos, and take the special function of the rhythm section into account.

Improvisation Ensembles

The "Improvisation Ensemble" lessons are meant to address any class that does not fit under the umbrella of concert band, orchestra, choir, or jazz ensemble. These lessons are meant to be flexible enough to address general music classes, secondary general music classes, music technology classes, keyboard classes, as well pop/rock ensembles. Although not completely unheard of, formal improvisation ensembles are relatively rare in K–12 schools. However, we encourage teachers to consider starting a free or group improvisation ensemble within their curricular or extracurricular options. These classes do not need to be completely "free," but as Hickey (2009) suggests, they can encapsulate "a balance between structure and freedom; a stance that balances teaching of skills (the current approach) along with encouraging freedom" (p. 286).

One of the great benefits of such an ensemble in the school setting is that there is no set instrumentation or repertoire, so *any* student of any musical experience level can participate. The lessons within this book would be a start for a structural approach, one that considers the musical elements that all students are able to explore. Moreover, the activities provide the freedom for students to explore these elements in personally meaningful ways and to draw conclusions and build new challenges with the teacher to develop overall musicianship.

Ensemble/Class Levels

This book includes lessons for beginner- and intermediate-level ensembles, with optional advanced extensions included in some of the intermediate lessons. The beginning lessons are designed with elementary and middle schools in mind, while the intermediate lessons are geared toward middle and high school students. However, we recommend that teachers use their own discretion in choosing lessons that are appropriate for their students. For instance, if this is the first time many high school students engage in improvisation activities, then starting with beginning-level improvisation activities may be more appropriate. The teacher can also modify class discussion with different levels of questioning that engage students in their specific level of musical understanding.

Structure of Lessons

We hope that by understanding the students' and teacher's role in improvisation as well as the benefits of practice, teachers are willing to explore the lesson plans included in Section III. Each lesson includes a description, materials, procedures, learning goals, assessments, learning benefits, and recordings or extra materials.

Description

The description of each lesson provides insights into the inspiration for lessons as well as a brief overview of the lesson activity and goals. Each description is succinct in order for the teacher to quickly evaluate the appropriateness of the activity for his or her ensemble.

Materials

Materials for the lesson do not refer to instruments, but rather other resources that enhance the lesson. These resources may include recordings, images, recording equipment suggestions, and so on. If recordings or images are needed, we provide a list of resources in the recording and resources section.

Procedure

Each procedure section includes a sequence for class activities with a summary of teacher and student responsibilities. We provide clear descriptions of sequenced steps, but also offer flexibility for adapting steps to meet students' needs.

Learning Goals

The learning goals section provides specific aims for the improvisation activity. Points in the lesson goals can fit into larger lesson goals as described in the learning benefits section.

Assessment

Each lesson includes both formative and summative suggestions for assessment. Some of the assessments focus on the improvisation itself, and other assessments help the teacher evaluate skills related to improvisation, such as students' listening ability, specific knowledge and skills for a particular genre, or the broad musical area (melody, harmony, rhythm, timbre and texture, articulation, and dynamics). However, it is important to note that assessment in improvisational teaching is incomplete without the crucial role teachers play in listening and providing ongoing, meaningful feedback.

Learning Benefits

The learning benefits section streamlines the positive aspects of teaching an improvisation activity into possible larger ensemble or class goals. For instance, an ensemble may have difficulty with balance, and a lesson within the texture/timbre section may help a group listen across the ensemble. Also, some activities may succeed in engaging hidden student possibilities and musical interactions. The brief points help teachers address why and how they should include an activity when their schedules may already seem quite full.

Recordings and Resources

This section provides recordings, videos, and images that may enhance the overall experience of the improvisation activity. The recordings are particularly vital in expanding students' musical vocabulary and providing contextual nuance for possibilities in improvisation. As many masterful improvisation pedagogues underscore, it is difficult to teach a particular "groove" or "feel" through direct instruction. Although not a substitute for live performance, guiding students toward relevant recordings provides them with a more authentic cultural context for their improvisations. Each of the lesson activities includes recording or video recommendations. It is important to note that these recordings are not meant to serve as a "blueprint" for the activity procedure. Instead, these recordings typically function as examples by masterful musicians that demonstrate a similar musical "ethos" to the lesson activity. Some of the activities include MP3 examples of the activity, as performed by a K–12 or university ensemble. These recordings can be accessed on our companion website. (Look for the web icon.) The recordings *are* intended to serve as a broad "road map" for the activity procedure. However, the teacher should remember that musical improvisation will inevitably lead in different directions for different musicians. With this purpose, the MP3 examples should be used as broad examples and not as strict guides. All recording and resource suggestions are simply the beginning of materials that could enhance the goals of the lesson. Teachers are encouraged to expand upon these ideas with their own resources.

Lessons

Melody

Beginning Instrumental/Choral Ensemble— *Limited Pitch Set*

Description

This activity loosely imitates one of the basic elements of Middle Eastern improvisation in a way that is useful for very young improvisers. For the activity, a teacher should write a limited set of pitches on the blackboard (in their respective transpositions) and the students should aim to improvise only with those pitches (octave changes are allowed). In Middle Eastern improvisation, players combine two maqams (tetrachords) to create the scale on which they improvise. They repeat, hold, and sequence notes. This activity is inspired by those principles but allows students to layer sound rather than work on extended melodic ideas.

Materials

If the lesson is taught visually, a handout, blackboard, whiteboard, or computer screen that contains the three to five notes of the limited pitch set.

Learning Goals

- Students will begin to explore the different combinations of melodic intervals produced by the pitch set.
- Students will begin to shape melodic roles for themselves in a group improvisation.
- Students will begin to use creative means for improvising with a limited pitch set. Such creative means might include timbre, dynamics, articulation, rhythm, and/or range.
- Students will begin to perceive how their individual melodies fit into the larger group texture.
- Students will begin to aurally identify pitch intervals based on the selected limited pitch set.

Procedure

Teachers supply students with a collection of three to five notes, either by displaying them visually or aurally. The teacher should instruct the students to improvise by using the designated pitch set. The teacher may elect to make range a variable and allow students to play the same notes in different octaves.

- Begin by giving students a minute or two to simply practice and explore the notes in the pitch set. This activity will probably be somewhat cacophonous, like a concert band warming up before the conductor lifts her baton for attention. The teacher should tell the students not to be discouraged: *This is the process, not the product.*
- The teacher can assign musical "roles" for each student or group of students which will make the activity seem less open ended and overwhelming. Examples of such "roles" with a three-to-five-note pitch set might include but are not limited to the following:
  - Long pedal notes
  - A repeating bassline
  - A repeating riff or counterline
  - A melodic figure
  - A rhythmic groove
- We recommend that the teacher follow the assignment of roles by demonstrating an example of each "role" with his instrument or voice. The teacher should ask the students to play back his example by ear and rote. See Figure 3.1 for examples of such musical "role" figures for a three-to-five-note pitch set.
  - If a student is nervous about improvising, he should be allowed to repeat the figure performed by the teacher. *Note: Students should be allowed to proceed at their own comfortable pace. Too much "forced" participation can discourage a student and cause her to "shut down" to the concept of improvisation.*
  - The teacher should frame the activity according to the rough skill level of the group of students. If the group is an advanced chamber choir, the teacher might encourage the students to explore a variety of musical "roles."
- After some exploration, the teacher should discuss how the same three to five notes can be used to create an interesting group improvisation. The teacher can also reassign or "trade up" musical "roles" to students so that they can experiment with different parts of the overall musical texture.
- Some of the terminology such as "pedal notes" and "counterlines" may be new for young students. In that case, the teacher should be ready to model these concepts with her instrument or voice.
- Depending on skill level and teaching goals, this activity can be used in two possible ways:
  - If the students have very limited musical experience, the activity can be framed to fit their current knowledge. For example, if the students know only four notes,

Limited Pitch Set

Examples based on pitch set: F, Ab, A, Bb

1. Long Pedal Notes
2. Repeating Bass Line
3. Repeating Riff
4. Melodic Counterline
5. Melody
6. Rhythmic Groove

FIGURE 3.1 Limited pitch set example

then there is nothing wrong with encouraging them to have fun improvising on a pitch set of those four notes.

- ○ This activity can also be used as a technique development challenge. The learning goal of the teacher may be to have the trumpeters expand their range, or have the choir manage bigger intervals better, or have the orchestra work on more complex finger patterns. In these cases, the teacher can frame the pitch sets so that they fit this challenge.

- Non-pitched percussion: These students can either be prompted to participate in the "Rhythmic Groove" role described previously or approximate the selected limited pitch set with a collection of drums with different timbres.

Assessment

Formative

- The teacher asks students to submit a recording of themselves (solo or with a group) performing this activity on pitches from a difficult arpeggio or scale. The teacher listens to the recordings, makes notes on student techniques used with limited pitch set, and adjusts future practice.
- The teacher asks students to perform or record themselves performing a limited pitch set drawn from a tricky technical passage in one of their concert pieces. The teacher listens to recordings, makes notes on student techniques used with limited pitch set, and adjusts future practice.

Summative

- If the activity is used for students to demonstrate mastery of certain notes or techniques, the teacher should assess and/or grade students on their performance of the notes or techniques utilized in the exercise in conjunction with the original version of the passage.

Lesson Benefits

- Beginning improvisers can explore without concern for an overwhelming number of musical options.
- Beginning improvisers can participate in group improvisation based on an agreed set of notes.
- The limited pitch set allows young improvisers to explore the rhythm, timbre, articulation, and dynamics in the context of a group improvisation.
- Students can creatively develop procedural "muscle" memory for difficult note passages.
- Students can practice aural discrimination of different pitch sets and intervals.

Recordings

- Artist: Ravi Shankar
- Recording: *Improvisations*

- Artist: Ravi Shankar
- Recording: *Live in 1972*

- Artist: Horace Silver (Soloist: Joe Henderson)
- Recording: *Song for My Father*
- *Note: This recording does not represent a strict or "pure" example of limited pitch set improvisation; however, Joe Henderson's remarkable saxophone solo demonstrates endless creative variations on a small collection of notes.*

Intermediate Instrumental/Choral Ensemble— *Brahmsian Improvisation*

Description

Johannes Brahms built on over four centuries of compositional devices to reimagine and extend musical ideas in his works. These devices include, for instance, fragmentation, transposition, inversion, retrograde, rhythmic diminution, and rhythmic augmentation. For this activity, the students will use the melodic and thematic devices exemplified by the composer Johannes Brahms to create a coherent group improvisation

Materials

Worksheet with sample melodic fragment ["Sample Thematic Transformations"], Figure 3.2 for pitched percussion, and Figure 3.3 for non-pitched percussion.

Learning Goals

- Students will explore the thematic development devices of Johannes Brahms and other composers.
- Students will learn to develop a given melody from a multifaceted perspective.

Procedure

- To begin, the teacher should select a simple melodic fragment. The fragment can either be from the ensemble's repertoire or not (we use the example of the "Shaker Theme" as borrowed by Aaron Copland for *Appalachian Spring* in Figure 3.2) but it should be simple and not too harmonically complex.
- The teacher should either print out the melody for students or teach it to them aurally by rote. The teacher should then play/sing the melody as written for the students and then demonstrate examples of the following devices: fragmentation, transposition, inversion, retrograde, rhythmic diminution, and rhythmic augmentation.
- The teacher should either ask for volunteers or select a group of students. The teacher should play or sing the original melody as part of a repeating vamp. One by one, students should enter the texture and improvise with fragments of the melody and liberally employ fragmentation, transposition, inversion, retrograde, rhythmic diminution, and/or rhythmic augmentation.
  - This exercise should be performed first in small groups, so students can hear the melodic ideas of their peers.
  - As always, students who are initially anxious about the task should not be pushed too hard. The teacher should allow any anxious students to play the original melody as written until they are ready to try a thematic transformation.
- See the example for "Sample Thematic Transformations" (Figure 3.2).

Sample Thematic Transformations

FIGURE 3.2 Sample Thematic Transformations (pitched instruments)

- Non-pitched percussion: Non-pitched instruments should attempt the transformations that work in a rhythmic setting such as diminution, augmentation, fragmentation, and retrograde. Students can also use non-pitched percussion instruments of different timbres and attempt to emulate a melodic transformation such as inversion as best as they can. For example, a percussionist can use the head of a snare drum, the rim of a snare drum, and a tom-tom drum as the three timbres that represent the "makeshift pitches." After determining an order and frequency for the timbres, the percussionist can apply the principles of thematic transformations. See Figure 3.3.
- *Advanced*—When the students begin to grow comfortable with this activity, the teacher can begin to have a larger group of students perform the activity by using more than one melody from a given piece of music. The teacher should keep in mind that the inclusion of more melodies might result in a more dissonant texture. The teacher should

Brahmsian Improvisation
[Non-Pitched Percussion Example]

FIGURE 3.3 Sample Thematic Transformations (non-pitched percussion)

tell the students that this dissonance is to be expected and that they should not shy away from experimenting and having fun.

Assessment

Formative

Students can write a reflection on this activity.

- The teacher can prompt one student or a group of a few students to record this activity on a program such as Garageband or Audacity. These programs are suggested because they allow a single student to "layer" multiple lines. The teacher provides

Thematic Checklist for Formative or Summative Assessment

Aim to get two out of the list:

_____ Augmentation.	Comments _____
_____ Diminution.	Comments _____
_____ Inversion.	Comments _____
_____ Retrograde.	Comments _____
_____ Fragmentation.	Comments _____
_____ Transposition.	Comments _____
_____ *Retrograde Inversion.	Comments _____

* Retrograde inversion is particularly challenging and a teacher may consider giving a student full credit if he or she successfully implements only this device.

FIGURE 3.4 *Assessment:* Brahmsian improvisation checklist

written feedback according to the thematic checklist (See Figure 3.4) to individuals on techniques used.

Summative

- On the basis of the thematic checklist (see Figure 3.4), the teacher grades individual student performance in a subsequent group recording.
- The teacher can prompt students to write a paper on Brahms's thematic practices or perform a thematic analysis of a work by Brahms or another composer.

Lesson Benefits

- Students can simultaneously practice thematic improvisation and learn about a key composition practice in music history.
- Instead of generating new melodic ideas from scratch, students can practice developing predetermined melodic themes.
- Students can practice melodic and textural improvisation unencumbered by the obstacles of harmonic movement and modulation.

Recordings

Please visit the Oxford University Press Companion Website for Listening Example 1.1 ▶ *of a high school wind ensemble performing this activity.*

- Artist: Johannes Brahms
- Recording(s): Almost any Brahms work would provide an expert demonstration. His Symphony No. 2 is a particularly excellent example.

- Artist: Aaron Copland
- Piece: *Appalachian Spring*

- Artist: Bill Holman Band
- Recording: *A View From the Side*

- Artist: Bill Holman Band
- Recording: *Brilliant Corners: The Music of Thelonious Monk*

- Artist: Sonny Rollins
- Recording: *Saxophone Colossus*
- Song: "Blue 7"
- *Note: Without a doubt, saxophonist Sonny Rollins was one of the greatest thematic improvisers of all time. Although real-time jazz improvisation does not give a soloist much of an opportunity to intentionally use the devices mentioned in this activity, "Blue 7" is a brilliant example of Rollins stretching a motif to its absolute limits. The solo was actually transcribed and formally analyzed by the famous classical/jazz composer, Gunther Schuller.*

Beginning Jazz Ensemble—*Melodic Ornamentation*

Description
The purpose of this activity is to have young jazz students imitate the great jazz improvisers who used ornamentation of the original melody as a melodic device. Such figures include Louis Armstrong, Lester Young, Thelonious Monk, Horace Silver, Sonny Rollins, and Max Roach.

Materials
Sheet music if the teacher decides to take a notated approach (versus an aural approach).

Learning Goals
- Students will practice ornamenting familiar melodies.
- Students will practice thematic development over familiar melodies.
- Students will memorize and develop deeper structural awareness of various melodies through ornamentation.
- Students will explore melodic ornamentation as an accessible and functional approach to improvisation.

Procedure
- The basic procedure of this lesson prompts the teacher to outline a melody for the students to use as a framework for ornamentation. This lesson is particularly suitable for a jazz ensemble, since melodic ornamentation represented the earliest seeds of jazz improvisation, and many extraordinary jazz musicians have demonstrated this technique.
- Although the teacher can certainly print out a written copy of the melody for the students, aural skills are particularly important to the practice of improvisation and thus we recommend that the teacher use a call-and-response approach to have the students slowly learn a melody by ear.

- There are two recommended approaches for melodic material:
  - Using simple or diatonic common/traditional melodies such as "Twinkle, Twinkle," "Happy Birthday," or "America the Beautiful"
  - Using the primary melody of a jazz ensemble "chart" or concert repertoire piece
    Note: Although both approaches are beneficial, the second approach has the added benefit of strengthening student awareness of the concert repertoire (particularly for the instrumentalists who do not have the main melody) while also developing improvisation skills.
- The teacher can then have the students perform a warm-up activity in which they play the melody, first exactly as performed by the teacher and then with variations.
- The teacher can demonstrate multiple melodic variations for the students, whether it is turning a quarter note into two swing eighth notes, changing a downbeat to an upbeat, or adding a grace note to an entrance.
- The teacher can structure this activity in various ways, depending on the length of the melody:
  - If the work has a short melody, such as a melody that is part of a 12-bar blues, then each student can have a turn playing the entire melody.
  - If the melody is longer, such as one that is part of a 32-bar AABA form, then the director might have the students each take turns playing four-measure or eight-measure sections of the melody.
    - *Note: This variation is particularly helpful for the drummer, who can learn how to use a melody as an excellent source for improvisational material. Drum set players should not be ignored, as they can benefit greatly from creatively performing melodic variations on their drum kit. In this activity, it is important to remember to include the rhythm section.*
  - This warm-up can also be used as the basis for a listening activity for the ensemble. The director can play recorded examples of artists such as Louis Armstrong, Lester Young, Thelonious Monk, Horace Silver, and Max Roach, demonstrating how seminal jazz improvisers have used variations on a tune's melody as the material for their own solos. It is important to note that having a jazz ensemble listen to many iconic jazz artists is incredibly valuable for the students. As a result, not only will students hear how great jazz artists approach improvisation, but this exercise will also reinforce the idea that each improviser performs melodies and improvisations differently. Finally, this activity will help students understand the workings of the repertoire better, particularly students who play instruments such as the baritone saxophone, bass trombone, and double bass, all of whom rarely get to play the melody.
  - This is an activity that should be repeated at several rehearsals. As a result, apprehensive students may become more comfortable with the idea of melodic

variation as they repeatedly hear different variations of the melody and begin to develop their own variations.

- It is very important to avoid criticizing students who are apprehensive about the activity and who play the melody or their section of the melody exactly as modeled. The director also must strenuously avoid criticizing students whose variations do not sound like the melody, as this is simply part of the experimentation process, and such student censorship should be avoided.

- *Advanced*—The idea of melodic ornamentation is not a new concept and some music teachers may already prompt students to participate in this activity. Although one can certainly never work on melodic ornamentation *too much*, two alternative activities that practice linear melodic awareness are listed. *Note: These are listed as more advanced activities because they require some basic knowledge of harmony and voice leading on the part of the students. These two options are a little less amenable to non-pitched percussion instruments.*

  o The teacher should prompt a student to perform basic stepwise voice leading based on the harmony of a given chord progression. The student should begin with basic whole-note and half-note rhythms. When they begin to feel comfortable with the process, they can begin to formulate more creative rhythms over the voice leading. Figure 3.5 includes an example that is based on the chord changes to "On Green Dolphin Street" by Bronislaw Kaper and Ned Washington.

  o The student should be encouraged to play the *exact same rhythm* repeatedly as a riff over the chord changes but to adjust the melodic content of the riff to fit the changing harmonies. This activity is somewhat similar to *Blues* and *Synchronicity* in this book. This concept is demonstrated over a 12-bar B♭ blues in Figure 3.6. *Note: Lester Young, Harry "Sweets" Edison, and Paul Desmond were masters of this approach in the jazz idiom.*

Assessment

Formative

- The teacher can informally assess students' melodic ornamentation improvisations in jazz ensemble through observation and verbal feedback.
- The teacher can prompt students to record themselves performing a melodic ornamentation over a melody extracted from their jazz ensemble repertoire or a culturally familiar melody. Teacher or peers can provide feedback on recordings.
- The teacher can prompt students to compose a melodic ornamentation over a melody extracted from their jazz ensemble repertoire or a culturally familiar melody. The teacher or peers can review the composed melodic ornamentations and provide suggestions.

FIGURE 3.5 Linear voice leading example over "On Green Dolphin Street"

Summative

- The teacher can prompt advanced students to transcribe an improvised solo (see recommended recordings) that makes use of melodic ornamentation. The teacher assesses transcriptions on the basis of melodic and rhythmic accuracy.
- Students can resubmit their composed melodic ornamentation over a melody extracted from their jazz ensemble repertoire or a culturally familiar melody. The teacher assesses whether the ornamentation falls within stylistic guidelines and or any other guidelines established by the class.

"On Green Dolphin Street"

FIGURE 3.5 Continued

Lesson Benefits

- Students can explore an accessible improvisation alternative to harmonic chord-change improvisation. Additionally, students do not require a serious background in jazz theory for this activity.
- Jazz students can explore an improvisation approach that has a deep tradition in jazz history, ranging from Louis Armstrong to Thelonious Monk.
- Jazz ensemble students can use this activity as a pathway to deeper structural understanding of repertoire and culturally familiar melodies.

Every measure includes a simple transposition of the 5th, ♭7th, and Root of the chord.

FIGURE 3.6 Rhythmic "cell" repetition over 12-bar blues

- While many students feel that they must improvise a solo "from scratch"—particularly by using the blues scale, pentatonic scales, or chord changes—this activity will demonstrate that incorporating a variation of the melody into jazz solos is an excellent way to perform an improvisation solo.

Recordings

- Artist: Sonny Rollins
- Recording: *Saxophone Colossus*
- Song: "Blue 7"

- Artist: Gabriela Montero
- Recording: *Baroque*

- Artist: Thelonious Monk
- Recording: *Monk's Dream* (almost any track from this recording)

- Artist: Thelonious Monk
- Recording: *Solo Monk* (almost any track from this recording)

- Artist: Louis Armstrong and Ella Fitzgerald
- Recording: *Ella and Louis*
- Song: Louis Armstrong's trumpet solo on "They Can't Take That Away From Me"
  *Note: Almost **any** Louis Armstrong solo works in this regard.*

- Artist: Kenny Dorham
- Recording: *Page One* [Joe Henderson is the leader for the date]
- Song: "Blue Bossa"

- Artist: Slam Stewart
- Recording: *Don Byas and Slam Stewart: Smithsonian Collection of Classic Jazz Volume 3*
- Song: Slam Stewart's bass solo on "I Got Rhythm"

- Artist: Stanley Jordan
- Recording: *Magic Touch*
- Song: Solo guitar work on "Eleanor Rigby"

- Artist: Max Roach
- Recording: *Bird's Best Bop on Verve*
- Song: Max Roach's drum solo on "Au Privave"

- Artist: Lester Young
- Recording: *Ken Burns Jazz*

- Artist: Harry "Sweets" Edison
- Recording: *Ben & Sweets*

- Artist: Dave Brubeck
- Recording: *Time Out* (listen for Paul Desmond's saxophone solos)

- Artist: Dave Brubeck
- Recording: *Jazz at Oberlin* (listen for Paul Desmond's saxophone solos)

Intermediate Jazz Ensemble—*Theory of Relativity*

Description

Many of our own students have stated that they are unnerved by jazz improvisation because of the challenge of keeping up with the chord changes. Improvising over chord changes is actually a very cognitively complex task. It involves extensive implicit theory knowledge, engendered cultural understanding, practiced technical facility, and acute listening skills. The purpose of this activity is to intentionally decontextualize the activity to remove the performance pressure for students and allow students to melodically explore common jazz scales.

Note: Chord-based jazz theory is mainly centered around linking the modes of the major scale and the melodic minor scale to specific chords and/or voicings.

Materials

Written examples of chord/scale relationships, Figure 3.7.

Learning Goals

- Students will learn the theoretical basics of chord/scale relationships.
- Students will explore the idiomatic characteristics of a given chord/scale without the pressure of improvising over chord changes in real time.
- Students will listen to chord/scale sounds and begin to aurally recognize certain harmonies.

Sample Jazz Chord/Scale Relationships

An F# Dorian scale (an E major scale starting on the second scale degree) can be used over an F# minor seventh chord.

A B Mixolydian scale (an E major scale starting on the fifth scale degree) can be used over a B dominant seventh chord.

*A B bebop scale can **also** be used over a B dominant seventh chord, particularly when used in a descending direction.*

An E major or Ionian scale can be used over an E major seventh chord.

FIGURE 3.7 Common jazz chord/scale relationships

Procedure

- The purpose of this activity is to give jazz students the opportunity to melodically explore a particular jazz scale without real-time chord-change pressures (in that way, this activity is very similar to "Flamenco Mittens with Strings" in the Harmony lessons). The teacher or director should try, as described in other parts of this book, to *streamline* this activity with the ensemble's concert and repertoire needs. For example, a high school jazz arrangement may include a ii–V⁷–I in a more difficult key, such as E or D♭ major. For this example, let us say that the jazz ensemble arrangement features a ii–V⁷–I in the key of E major. The teacher would demonstrate the F♯ minor seventh (ii⁷) chord with a minor seventh arpeggio. *Note: As was stated several times in this text, a teacher can teach this component visually or aurally. The teacher must gauge his or her particular situation. A written/visual approach typically allows the activity to move forward faster, while an aural approach better simulates the nature of music as an aural art form.* The teacher will then demonstrate the corresponding F♯ Dorian scale that is part of the recommended chord/scale relationship.

- The teacher should have the rhythm section vamp on an F♯ minor seventh chord. The rhythm section should not vamp on the same thing over and over. This activity should be used as an opportunity for the following:
  - The pianist/guitarist to explore different minor seventh voicings.
  - The bassist to explore different notes over a minor seventh chord.
  - The drummer to explore different textures and colors.
- All or some of the students in the ensemble will simultaneously explore an F♯ Dorian scale over the rhythm section vamp. Simultaneously, group playing will help keep individual students from becoming self-conscious. The teacher should remind the students that the goal is to explore; there should be no pressure to play anything impressive.
- After performing this activity with the F♯ minor seventh chord, the teacher should perform the same activities with the B dominant seventh chord and the E major seventh chord. The B^7 chord is a good example of a chord for which the students can practice either a B Mixolydian scale or a B bebop scale or both.
- As the students begin to gain facility with these chords, the activity can begin to use the procedure of "Flamenco Mittens with String" from this book. The rhythm section can randomly (but slowly) transition from one chord in the ii–V^7–I to the next. For example, the rhythm section might vamp on the ii^7 chord for 10 beats but then vamp on the V^7 chord for 14 beats. The purpose of this activity is to have the students simultaneously practice a given scale without the real-time pressures of chord changes *and* to develop their aural jazz skills. This activity imitates the "modal" or extended scale improvisation found on classic jazz recordings such as *Kind of Blue* and *My Favorite Things.*

Advanced: While this activity attempts to address a relaxed exploration of chord/scale relationships, it does not immediately address the *harmonic voice leading* used by most jazz greats to link or bridge two different chords. The ability to confidently execute this type of voice leading typically requires some basic knowledge in "upper extension" harmony, or the 9th, 11th, or 13th of a given chord. Many professional jazz musicians create interesting voice leading and non-chord tones colors with the ♭9, ♯9, ♯11, or ♭13. As part of the advanced form of this activity, the "soloist" student will solo on a given chord and the teacher will conduct a "pivot" into the next chord change, allowing the student to practice chromatic voice leading techniques. See Figure 3.8.

Assessment

Formative

- The teacher can prompt students to record themselves performing the arpeggios and scales for the chord changes for a particular jazz ensemble piece. The teacher can

FIGURE 3.8 "Theory of Relativity" pivot note example

informally give verbal or written feedback on student progress, or students can self-assess their recordings and share with peers.

- The teacher can prompt students to get together with a member or members of the rhythm section and record themselves performing the activity in a soloist capacity. Students should review recordings at home to self-assess their alignment with the rhythm section and share those reflections in class.

Summative

- As students begin to gain traction with the activity, they can submit a chord/scale diagram for a set of "standard" chord changes (in the most general sense, "standard" refers to a commonly performed Broadway/Tin Pan Alley song or jazz composition). The teacher can grade this submission on the basis of accuracy.
- After enough practice with this activity, the teacher can prompt students to record themselves improvising over the chord changes in real time, either with a live rhythm section or a play-along recording. Students can review recordings at home to self-assess their alignment with the chord changes and write a reflection on it for the teacher. The teacher assesses the detail and accuracy of students' reflections on their performance.

Lesson Benefits

- Students can practice jazz chord/scale relationships without real-time tempo pressures.
- Students can explore chord/scale sounds as a group without being isolated in front of their peers.

Recordings
- Artist: Herbie Hancock
- Recording: *Maiden Voyage*

- Artist: John Coltrane
- Recording: *My Favorite Things*
- Song: "My Favorite Things"

- Artist: Hilary Hahn and Hauschka
- Recording: *Silfra*

- Artist: Miles Davis
- Recording: *Kind of Blue*

- Artist: Kenny Wheeler
- Recording: *Gnu High*

Beginning Improvisation Ensemble—*Light Motif*
Description
The purpose of this activity is to have students improvise melodies that are inspired by external references. The choice of the references is up to the teacher. They can include paintings, poems, stories, or movies. The title is a play on Richard Wagner's famous use of "leitmotifs" with musical drama characters and actions.

Materials
Any materials (a painting slide show, a poem, a story, a movie, etc.) that yield recognizable themes, preferably recurring themes.

Learning Goals
- Students will begin to develop a thematic approach to improvisation.
- Students will begin to develop awareness of historical thematic approaches to composition and improvisation.
- Students will develop experience spontaneously reacting to external referents.
- Students will develop experience integrating their individual improvised themes into a larger group texture.

Procedure
The teacher should first select a painting, poem, story, or movie that includes recurring themes (preferably several). An effective musical model would be a ballet or other musical works that use specific musical themes to represent elements of the story (two obvious examples are *The Nutcracker Suite* or *Peter and the Wolf*). *Note: Since paintings are "static" in terms of direct movement or progression, we recommend that the teacher set up a timed slide*

show presenting a series of paintings that follow a theme. Examples might include a series of paintings based on nature or a series of paintings on similar themes painted by the same artist, such as Monet and water lilies, Degas and ballet dancers, or O'Keefe and flowers.

- We recommend that the teacher use a work that is familiar with students. This is where interdisciplinary collaboration can be potent. Opening a dialogue with literature or art teachers can pave the way for a musical exploration of works studied in other school classes. The referenced work might be a filmed production of a Shakespeare play studied in a literature class or a unit on landscape paintings in art class. The key to the activity's success is that the work or collection of works represents multiple recurring themes.
- Depending on the size of a given class or group, a work may have fewer themes or characters than students. If that is the case, we recommend that the teacher assign a given theme or character to a small group of students, who should be encouraged to conference and construct a musical idea that embodies the given theme. If students are apprehensive about improvising a motif, they can select a section from their repertoire (popular music or class pieces) that represents the character of the theme. For example, a student might select a sprightly Top 40 melody to go with the character of Puck in *A Midsummer Night's Dream*. Each small group of students should be encouraged to perform the musical idea spontaneously and interactively, listening for one another's interpretations and bouncing ideas off one another.
- In the beginning stages, it might be a good idea for the teacher to suggest a key or tonal area and a rough tempo. It will be very difficult for new group improvisers to musically connect while simultaneously referencing an external theme without some set boundaries.
- Once this process is complete, the referenced work should be played or performed and students should be prompted to play their "assigned" theme with each appearance or entrance.
  - It is up to the student to spontaneously adjust the performance of this theme on the basis of the character or nature of the theme's presentation in the work. The beauty of artistic expression is that the same theme can be evoked through different expressions. For example, in the Li-Young Lee (1986) poem, "Persimmons," the idea of 'yarn' takes on two different meanings: A source of embarrassment and confusion for an individual who is a new English speaker, and a source of limitless possibilities for an inspired poet.
  - Furthermore, the beauty of Wagner's "leitmotifs" was that different themes can interact in different ways in a given work of art. For example, students playing musical ideas that represent two film characters might perform the two ideas differently, depending on if the characters are arguing or flirting.
  - Examples of ways that students can "color" themes include but are not limited to the following:
    - Adjust the dynamic performance of the musical idea on the basis of the mood of the theme's presentation.

- Adjust the articulation of the musical idea.
- Adjust the tempo of the musical idea.
- Change the range in which the musical idea is performed (higher/lower).
- Adjust the timbre of the musical idea.
- Extend the musical idea or add more melodic content.
- Play a small fragment of the musical idea.
- Transpose the musical idea into a new key.

Assessment

Formative

- The teacher can prompt students to write a brief reflection on their approach to improvising a musical theme from an external referent (examples include but are not limited to movies, paintings, books, a particular view of a city, or nature). The teacher reviews students' responses for future planning.
- The teacher can prompt students to record a musical "soundtrack" for a work and use a program such as iMovie or YouTube to insert the recorded improvisation as a musical soundtrack/accompaniment. Peers can provide feedback to one another about the alignment of the music to the video.

Summative

- The teacher can teach a lesson and/or assign a quiz/report on thematicism in the Romantic Era (e.g., Wagner, Strauss, Tchaikovsky, or Berlioz). Grading is based on the students' ability to identify or define thematic concepts and material of the Romantic Era.

Lesson Benefits

- Students can focus on thematic improvisation, shifting focus away from melodic, harmonic, and/or rhythmic pressures.
- Students can use external referents as inspiration for recurring improvisation themes.

Recordings

- Artist: Richard Wagner
- Work: Any of the four operas from *The Ring Cycle* or *Der Ring des Nibelungen*

- Artist: Hector Berlioz
- Work: *Symphony fantastique*

- Artist: Pyotr Ilyich Tchaikovsky
- Work: *The Nutcracker Suite*

- Artist: Pyotr Ilyich Tchaikovsky
- Work: *Swan Lake*

- Video Recording/DVD: Disney's *Fantasia*

Intermediate Improvisation Ensemble—*Middle Eastern Taqsim*

Description

The purpose of this exercise is to experiment with some of the organizing principles in Middle Eastern taqsim (improvisation). It is out of the purview of this book to cover Arabic maqam or the theory underlying this improvisational culture, but instead this lesson is inspired by some of the underlying structures of repetition; freedom from meter; sequence; and melodic contour that make taqsim entrancing and beautiful. The lesson is also inspired by the work of jazz violinist, Martin Norgaard (2016), and his approach to scalar improvisation.

Materials

If students do not have the prerequisite experience of playing the natural minor scale, the teacher can to print out a copy of this scale for students to reference.

Learning Goals

- Students will play a natural minor scale.
- Students will improvise on the natural minor scale by using repetition and sequence.
- Students will understand some of the basic organizing principles of Middle Eastern taqsim.
- Students will improvise by using the guidelines of a basic melodic contour found in Middle Eastern taqsim.

Procedure

- The teacher should divide the ensemble into two groups: one group to play a drone, and another to improvise on a natural minor scale. Seat students in pairs, with one playing a drone and the other improvising, so that the students can engage in spontaneous interaction. Three steps are suggested, and each partner should take a turn working through the steps while the other drones.
- First principle: Repetition and freedom from meter. The teacher should have one half of the group drone on the tonic of the scale, while the other half plays up and down the minor scale in consecutive order. The improvising group may repeat a single pitch in the scale as many times as they would like, or hold a pitch as long as they would like before moving on to the next pitch. The improvising group should begin on the tonic, go all the way up to the octave, and return to the tonic. Improvisers will end at different times, and as they end they should all drone on the tonic with their partner.
- Second principle: Sequence. Students should create a motive with no more than three pitches. Motifs with step motion and small leaps are easier to work with for beginner improvisers. Students should practice moving up and down the scale, applying the motif to consecutive scale degrees. Students should experiment with the tempo of their

sequence, moving quickly and slowly as they ascend and descend. Students experiment with this as their partner drones.

- Third principle: Melodic contour. A taqsim is generally built around a melodic contour that emphasizes the following scale degrees: I, IV, or V (depending upon the *maqam*); and the octave; before quickly descending and returning to the tonic. Students can use repetition and sequence to emphasize these pitches. For instance, a player might start by circling around tonic with the use of stepwise motion and playing the tonic repeatedly at different rates. The player would then move upward with sequence or repetition on consecutive scale degrees and emphasize the fifth. From the fifth, the improviser would take the same approach to the octave before quickly descending with a sequence back to the tonic. Figure 3.9 is a visualization of the emphases that happen in the melodic contour inspired by the teaching of Wanees Zarour (2012). One can see the circling of the melodic line around the tonic, the fourth and fifth degrees, and the octave.

- As students improvise, they should feel free to structure their improvisations with repetition and sequences as they would like.

- As students become comfortable with these basic principles, they should listen to Middle Eastern taqsim to hear how ornamentation is used to enhance and emphasize the melodic structure. Encourage students to explore trills, slides, and tempo to further develop their taqsims.

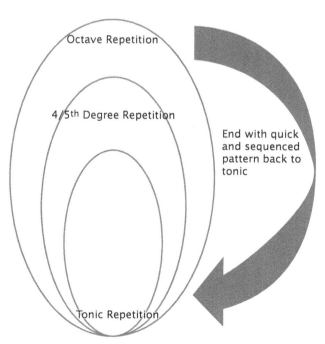

FIGURE 3.9 Visualization of taqsim

	5	4	3	2	1
Freedom from Meter	Meter is flexible, and space is used freely.	Meter is sometimes flexible and space is used freely.	Meter is sometimes flexible, but there is no use of space.	Student explores two meters, with no use of space.	Student plays completely in one meter with no use of space.
Repetition	Student uses a wide variety of ways to repeat pitches, and repeats all notes in melodic contour.	Student uses some variety in ways to repeat notes and repeats some of the resting notes in the melodic contour.	Student uses some variety in ways to repeat pitches, and repeats one of the resting notes in the melodic contour.	Student repeats some pitches, but never any of the resting notes in the melodic contour.	Student does not repeat any pitches.
Sequence	Student sequences step and small interval patterns masterfully, ascending and descending.	Student sequences short step patterns masterfully ascending and descending.	Student sequences patterns well either ascending or descending.	Student attempts sequencing either ascending or descending, but has difficulty holding onto a pattern.	Student does not attempt any sequencing.
Contour	There is a clear linear emphasis of the tonic, 4/5th degree, and octave before returning to tonic.	There is some linear emphasis of all but one of the following degrees: tonic, 4/5th degree, octave & tonic.	There is some linear emphasis on all but two of the following degrees: tonic, 4/5th degree, octave, & tonic.	Student emphasizes one of the degrees and has a general linear contour.	Student does not emphasize any of the degrees and has no ascending or descending linear contour.
Musicality (dynamics, ornamentation, timbre)	Student demonstrates excellent musicianship using a variety of dynamics, ornamentation, and timbres.	Student demonstrates strong musicianship demonstrating a variety of dynamics, ornamentation, and timbres.	Student demonstrates some musicianship skill using at least two of following: dynamics, ornamentation, and timbre.	Student demonstrates some musicianship skills using at least one of the following: dynamics, ornamentation, and timbre.	Student does not include any changes in dynamics, ornamentation, or timbre.

FIGURE 3.10 *Assessment*: Middle Eastern Taqsim rubric

Assessment

Formative

- The teacher prompts each student to describe how his or her partner used the organizing principles of sequence, repetition, and melodic contour to develop an improvisation with each other. Students write down points on paper for the improviser and the teacher to review.

- After students have practiced in the classroom, the teacher prompts students to record themselves playing a taqsim over a drone (students can easily find examples of drones on YouTube and elsewhere online or they can record their own drone on Garageband or Audacity) and to upload the recording to an online course tool. Students self-assess their performances in relation to the rubric (Figure 3.10).

Summative

- The teacher asks students to select their favorite recording of themselves improvising over a drone. The teacher assesses the recording by using the rubric (Figure 3.10).

Lesson Benefits

- Students improvise in a minor tonality and experience organizing principles of Middle Eastern taqsim while moving away from the constraints of meter.

Recordings

Please visit the Oxford University Press Companion Website for *Listening Examples 2.1* ⏵, a teacher modeling a taqsim while a student drones, and *Listening Example 2.2* ⏵, a student improvising while the teacher drones.

- Artist: Rahim Alhaj on Oud (traditional string instrument)
- Recording: *When the Soul Is Settled: Music of Iraq*
- Piece: "Taqsim Maqām Bayyat-Husayni"

- Artists: Armen Stepanyan on Duduk (traditional woodwind instrument)
- Recording: *Ancient Lands: Traditional Duduk Music From Armenia*
- Piece: "Quail"

- Composer: Javier Limón (for modern fusion interpretation)
- Recording: *Promesas de Tierra*
- Piece: "Promesas de Tierra"

- Artist: Naseem Alatrash with Michigan Arab Orchestra
- Example of Cello Taqsim
- Video: https://www.youtube.com/watch?v=9_z4jKdVINc

Harmony

Beginning Instrumental/Choral Ensemble—*Mood Music*

Description

The purpose of this activity is to create a pressure-free environment that encourages students to explore scales and chord arpeggios in a group improvisation setting. For this activity, the teacher will pick a particular key (e.g., concert F major). The teacher will break the ensemble up into groups and have different groups improvise with the root of the chord, the scale tones, and the arpeggio tones, respectively.

Materials

Scale/arpeggio sheets.

Learning Goals

- Students will begin to memorize and internalize different scales and arpeggios.
- Students will experience exploring scales and arpeggios in a spontaneous, creative setting.
- Students will explore textural group improvisation in a pressure-free setting.

Procedure

- The teacher should decide on a particular key, such as concert F major (it might be helpful for the teacher to write the scale on the board).
- The teacher should designate three different groups for the students:
  - A group that stays on the root of the chord (such as concert F)
  - A group that plays the scale (e.g., concert F major scale). *Each student in the group determines his own scale direction; the activity does not require unison linear movement.*

- A group that plays the arpeggio (e.g., concert F-major triad) in any direction. *Each student in the group determines her own linear direction; the activity does not require unison linear movement.*
- On the basis of the novelty of the activity and the general apprehension and attitude of the students, the teacher can opt for one of three different approaches to rhythm:
  - If the students are initially reluctant to exercise personal autonomy on this task, the teacher can initially assign a uniform rhythm for each group.
  - Each group can take five minutes and decide on a uniform rhythm for that group.
  - Each student can contribute his own individual rhythms.
- *Note: It is important that the students should be encouraged to pick their own group. They do not need to tell the teacher which group they choose and they should not feel pressured to coalesce with other members of their group. Each student should improvise anything she wants within the guidelines of the group. The activity is named mood music because the uniform key tends to keep the group from sounding too dissonant and cacophonous and the aural result is often reminiscent of the rhythmic murkiness and tranquility often associated with the genre known as "mood music."*
- If some students are particularly enthusiastic about this activity and want to take it a step further, they should be encouraged to join a fourth group: a group in which students solo freely over the assigned key without being assigned to roots, scale tones, or arpeggio tones.

Non-Pitched Percussion: Unfortunately, non-pitched percussion instruments will not be able to participate in the harmonic content of the exercise. Students who perform these instruments should be encouraged to imitate, interact with, or complement the rhythmic approach of a given group. *Note: Drummer Tony Williams's performance on the Miles Davis album "Nefertiti" is a perfect example of this approach.*

Assessment

Formative

- The teacher prompts students to write a brief reflection of the activity and how they can improve the aesthetic quality of this kind of performance. Students share that feedback with their peers.
- The teacher can prompt students to form a smaller group and try recording this activity with a new key/tonality. Students write a reflection on the recording and the teacher reviews the reflection. The teacher provides feedback and adapts future teaching to meet students' needs.
- The teacher can prompt ambitious students to take a recording of the ensemble performing this activity and record themselves soloing over the recording in a play-along/music-minus-one setting. The teacher provides individual verbal or written feedback to the soloists.

Summative

- The teacher prompts students to write a paper on one of the artists listed in the "Recordings" section and how that artist used harmony to achieve mood. The paper is graded on the students' ability to apply what they have learned in class to their listening and description of the recording.

Lesson Benefits

- Students can explore and internalize scales and arpeggios in a creative, spontaneous manner.
- Students can participate in group improvisation in a number of roles without the pressure of solo improvisation.

Recordings

Please visit the Oxford University Press Companion Website Listening Example 3.1 ⏵ *for an example of an elementary school concert band performing this activity.*

- Artist: Paul Winter Consort
- Album: *Canyon*

- Artist: Paul Motian Trio
- Album: *I Have the Room Above Her*

- Artist: Miles Davis Quintet
- Album: *Nefertiti*
- Song: "Nefertiti" (This track actually has a fascinating backstory. The quintet wanted to warm up on the tune before recording it for the album. The group practiced playing the Wayne Shorter melody several times in a row in many different styles. Fortunately, the studio was recording the proceedings and the rhythm section's accompaniment of the melody has become legendary. The warm-up ended up being the take of choice for Miles Davis on the recording.)

- Artist/Composer: Eric Whitacre
- Album: *Light & Gold*

- Artist: Paul Motian Trio
- Album: *It Should've Happened a Long Time Ago*
- Song: "It Should've Happened a Long Time Ago"

- Composer: Benjamin Britten
- Work: "First Sea Interlude" from the opera *Peter Grimes*

- Artist: Hilary Hahn and Hauschka
- Recording: *Silfra*

- Composer: György Ligeti
- Work: *Lux Aeterna* (This piece features some microtonal activity that will not be directly applicable to the activity; however, it perfectly illustrates how slowly an ensemble can move through note changes.)

Intermediate Instrumental/Choral Ensemble— *Celestial Navigation*

Description

The purpose of this activity is to encourage students to explore intonation, tone, and harmonic intervals as part of an extended long-tone activity. The title, "Celestial Navigation," comes from the ethereal sounds often produced when students explore simultaneous long tones. Although this activity has several musical benefits, a key benefit involves intonation awareness. When attempting to correct their personal intonation, many students simply look at a chromatic tuner and adjust accordingly. While the chromatic tuner is a terrific reference tool, overusing it skips a key component: *exploring the sounds, feelings, and vibrations of being in tune, sharp, or flat.*

Materials

Suggested recordings and a starting pitch or chord for reference.

Learning Goals

- The students will explore and "feel" various intonation settings on their particular instruments or voice.
- The students will explore and "feel" intonation settings on various musical intervals.
- The students will explore and "feel" intonation settings in various ranges.
- Students will gain cognitive and instrumental familiarity with different melodic intervals.

Procedure

- The teacher can introduce this activity by playing the suggested recordings that capture the awe and vastness of the cosmos. Together, teacher and students can reflect on techniques and effects that are used to musically interpret celestial views. The teacher then introduces this activity as one possible way to capture ethereal sounds that might depict the cosmos.
- The teacher should have the students begin by sustaining a long tone on a given note. If the students sing or play wind instruments, the teacher should tell them to stagger breath. The teacher should tell the students to sustain a stable sound for eight beats or so and then they should begin to experiment with their own intonation on that note. *Note: To experiment on this activity simply means that each student should move his or her own pitch up and down and simply listen and soak in the sound.* At the beginning of this exercise, students may find it helpful for the teacher to create a gesture indicating that they begin to stretch away from the primary intonation. The stretch should be very slow. The teacher can also gesture to slowly come back in tune.

- After this step, the teacher should expand the activity to include a major third and a perfect fifth (to form a major triad). The teacher should tell the students to alternate, at their own discretion, between the root, third, and fifth in whatever range they want. The students should also be encouraged to experiment with the intonation by moving the pitch up and down on whatever part of the chord they choose. This exercise will allow the students to listen to and absorb the different intonation sounds and vibrations as part of different intervals and harmonies. The next step should be for the teacher to extend the practice to include the major seventh and major ninth.
- As the students' comfort grows, the final step can be for the students to experiment with the intonation of any possible interval or harmony. For this step of the activity, we recommend that a rotating group of students be assigned to the root of the chord to keep the malleable harmony from modulating.
- Throughout this activity, students should carefully use dynamics to highlight dissonances and consonances.
- For a culminating activity, students can be invited to use the techniques from this activity to musically interpret a clip from *2001: A Space Odyssey* or images such as Vincent Van Gogh's *Starry Night,* photos of the Milky Way or Northern Lights, or images from the story of Antoine de Saint-Exupéry's *The Little Prince*. Students can be split into smaller groups to musically interpret an image/movie clip or several images. Students can also be encouraged to explore and experiment with texture, timbre, and dynamics.

Assessment

Formative

- The teacher can prompt students to record and document their progress tuning major-scale intervals. Their recordings and reflections can be uploaded to a school website, where the teacher can monitor students' progress.

Summative

- Students record their musical interpretation of celestial images or movie clips. They journal and reflect upon how their improvised performance captures the colors, depth, breadth, and majesty of outer space as depicted through their visual works. The teacher assesses the depth of students' reflections on their performances and connections to the visual works.
- *Advanced extension*: The music teacher connects with a teacher of the natural sciences or astrology, who describes to the ensemble the phenomena associated with celestial colors and movements. The discussion can even be geared toward specific images of the Northern Lights or the Milky Way. Next, students are challenged to bring their understanding of these phenomena into the musical interpretations of their images/movie clips. Students are then graded on their ability to connect their musical performances to the colors, depth, and breadth within images and how they also captured some of the celestial phenomena as described by the natural science/astrology teacher.

Lesson Benefits

- Students can internalize intonation through exploration and discovery learning.
- Students can improvise within a very delineated frame without musical isolation.
- Students can creatively explore the different textures of different pitch frequencies and interval combinations in a group improvisation texture.
- Students can learn the components of different scales and arpeggios through creative improvisation.

Recordings and/or Resources

Please visit the Oxford University Press Companion Website for an example of a high school chamber choir performing this activity. Listening Example 4.1 ⊙ is an example of students performing the activity on a unison note. Listening Example 4.2 ⊙ is an example of students performing the activity on a major triad.

- Artist: Jane Ira Bloom
- Recording: *Art & Aviation*

- Composer: Gustav Holst
- Work: *The Planets*
- Movement: "Neptune, the Mystic"

- Artist: Miles Davis
- Recording: *In a Silent Way*

- Artist: Peter Gabriel
- Recording: *So*
- Song: "Mercy Street"

- Composer: David Bedford
- Work: *12 Hours of Sunset*

- Composer: Karlheinz Stockhausen
- Work: *Stimmung*

- Composer: György Ligeti
- Work: *Lux Aeterna* (This piece features some microtonal activity that will not be directly applicable to the activity; however, it perfectly illustrates how slowly an ensemble can move.)

Films

- Title: *2001: A Space Odyssey*
- Director: Stanley Kubrick
- Film Score: The film uses various late Romantic and 20th century symphonic works by composers such as Richard Strauss, Johann Strauss II, and György Ligeti.

- Title: *Close Encounters of the Third Kind*
- Director: Steven Spielberg
- Film Score: John Williams

- Title: *Interstellar*
- Director: Christopher Nolan
- Film Score: Hans Zimmer

- Title: *Gravity*
- Director: Alfonso Cuarón
- Film Score: Steven Price

Beginning Jazz Ensemble—*Blues*

Description

The blues is fundamental not only to jazz but also to many other genres of American music. Many elementary and secondary jazz ensemble students begin blues improvisation with little or no foundational background in the blues, forcing many of them to nervously "grasp at straws," much as a driver does when lost in an unfamiliar neighborhood. The purpose of this activity is to use an improvisational approach to acclimate students with the harmonic and form-based foundations of the blues. More specifically, the students are asked to improvise basic background riffs on the root and, subsequently, other parts of the blues harmonies.

Materials

The teacher can begin with a basic Roman numeral chart or chord change lead sheet for the blues, but the teacher should eventually transition to aural practice so that the students can fully absorb the harmonies and form of the blues.

Learning Goals

- Students will learn the basic form of a 12-bar blues.
- Students will learn the harmonic foundations of the 12-bar blues.
- Students will learn to craft simple backgrounds that fit the harmonic form of a 12-bar blues.

Procedure

- Prior to performing the activity, the teacher should take some time and outline the harmonic fundamentals of the 12-bar blues. We recommend that the teacher explain this concept in terms of Roman numerals, as many students who have experienced only notated performance may not immediately grasp that the 12-bar blues form is virtually the same in any key (i.e., the Roman numerals do not change). See Figure 3.11 for an example of this explanation.

	I^7		IV^7		I^7		I^7	
	IV^7		IV^7		I^7		I^7	
	V^7		IV^7		I^7		V^7	

or

	I^7		IV^7		I^7		I^7	
	IV^7		IV^7		I^7		I^7	
	ii^{min7}		V^7		I^7		V^7	

FIGURE 3.11 Sample 12-bar blues form

- After finishing this explanation, the teacher should begin by picking a friendly key (e.g., concert B♭, E♭, F) and ask the students to play whole notes on the roots of the chords of the blues. *Note: It is critical that the teacher be patient with the students and invite their questions. Many students who have played only notation will find even this seemingly basic task to be daunting. Many will experience a type of "cognitive overload" because they have not had experience in such elements as chord construction, music theory, and tune form. Furthermore, many students will pretend as if they understood the directions when they do not understand, so the teacher should be sure to be friendly and inviting of questions.*
- For the next step, the teacher should play a sample measure-long rhythm for the students. Unless the teacher has specific background rhythms he or she wants to use, we recommend that the teacher use a rhythm from the "Jazz Rhythm Syllabus," Figure 3.12. The teacher should then demonstrate how the background rhythm should be performed on the root of each of the chords in a 12-bar blues. It may be difficult for some wind players to find a place to breathe in this activity, so the teacher should tell the students to skip measures whenever they need to breathe.
- The teacher should let the students get comfortable with this approach. There should not be a rush to move on to the next step. Many students are eager to close the door on jazz harmony because of confusion, mistakenly thinking they "aren't any good at it." The teacher should instinctively feel out his students and determine when they are ready to move on to a next step.
- For the next part, the students should stay on the roots of the blues harmonies but they should be invited to come up with their own measure-long rhythms. After an individual student creates a rhythm, the band should be invited to play her background rhythm together over the roots of the chords.
- When the teacher feels that the band is ready, he can feel free to move the same activity concept to the third, fifth, and seventh of the chord. *Note: The teacher should take special care to patiently explain the concept of a dominant seventh chord, most notably that the chord features a minor seventh and not a major seventh. This distinction will confuse many students who are used to playing a major scale with a major seventh. See* Figure 3.13 *for an example of this concept, using the different parts of the chords.*

Jazz Rhythm Syllabus

*Created by Chris Madsen and Daniel Healy

FIGURE 3.12 "Jazz Rhythm Syllabus"

- If the teacher is having students take individual solos over the blues (using the blues scale or other approaches), we recommend that the group consistently use this activity as a "background" for the solo. This practice will help the students develop some procedural knowledge for the 12-bar blues form.

Assessment

Formative

- The teacher can prompt students to record themselves improvising a blues chorus or two based on this activity. Students can write reflections on their ability to play over the blues form and the teacher can review reflections for future planning.

FIGURE 3.13 Jazz rhythm examples on different parts of chord

- The teacher can engage students in discussion that compares different blues forms (i.e., one with a V⁷–IV⁷–I⁷ ending and another with a ii⁷–V⁷–I⁷ ending) and consider their responses for future planning.

Summative

- Students can write a paper on a famous performer who played the blues, whether it is a blues, rock, or jazz performer, and discuss unique ways that the performer played over the blues form. The teacher assesses the student on his attention to detail and the quality of the writing.

Lesson Benefits

- Students learn to craft simple improvisatory lines over the blues.
- Students learn about the harmonic components of the blues.
- Students learn about the form of the blues.

Recordings

Note: Classic big band recordings provide great examples of simple background lines and riffs.

- Artist: Count Basie Orchestra
- Recording: *Chairman of the Board*
- Song: "Blues in Hoss Flat"

- Artist: Count Basie Orchestra
- Recording: *April in Paris*
- Song: "Corner Pocket"

- Artist: Woody Herman Orchestra
- Song: "Woodchopper's Ball" (Woody Herman's recorded output is notoriously scattered, particularly on CDs. This particular 12-bar blues song can be found on many Woody Herman compilation recordings, including *The Best of Woody Herman*).

Intermediate Jazz Ensemble—*Flamenco Mittens with String*

Description

Improvising over chord changes can feel amazingly difficult for secondary school jazz students. Not only does successful chord-change improvisation involve habitually internalized physical techniques and cognitive knowledge, but also students often understandably complain that the changes "move too fast!" This activity works to alleviate that stress by borrowing concepts from two classic jazz recordings: "Flamenco Sketches" from Miles Davis' *Kind of Blue* album, and John Coltrane's arrangement of the classic Rodgers and Hammerstein show tune "My Favorite Things" (Coltrane's album also goes by the name *My Favorite Things*).

Materials

Many published jazz ensemble pieces feature solo chord changes for only a few instruments. If the teacher wishes to extend this activity to the rest of the ensemble (certainly a good idea!), that teacher can print out a copy of the chord changes for all the instruments.

Learning Goals

- Students will have ample time to explore chord/scale relationships and, more importantly, experiment with sounds over a given harmony.

- Students will begin to internalize chord/scale relationships with some degree of automaticity so that they can begin to focus more on swing, groove, sound, and creativity during their own jazz solos.

Procedure

- To prep for the activity, the teacher should select the chord changes from any one of the arrangements in the jazz ensemble's repertoire. The teacher is encouraged to print up the piece's chord changes for all of the musicians in the band.
- If the teacher wants extra conceptual reinforcement, she can play the recordings of "Flamenco Sketches" and "My Favorite Things" for the students.
- The key component of the activity is that the rhythm section students should play each individual chord/harmony for as long as they wish. As with the aforementioned recordings, the soloist should improvise over that single chord change until the rhythm section moves on to the next one *(Note: This part of the activity is very similar to the advanced version of "The Theory of Relativity," as described in this book.)*

Activity Notes

- The rhythm section students should use listening and eye contact to determine when they should move on to the next chord in the sequence. If the students feel overwhelmed by this step, they can feel free to play each chord for a specific number of beats; however, we feel that this practice is actually more difficult than using listening and eye contact.
- If the rhythm section students are not very experienced in terms of creating their own basslines or piano/guitar voicings, they can feel free to simply repeat what is notated in the piece for a given chord/harmony. That being said, this activity is a *perfect* opportunity for these students to explore constructing their own basslines and voicings.
- The soloist should listen to determine when the rhythm section has proceeded to the next chord/harmony. If this task is too daunting for the soloist, the teacher should feel free to signal each chord change. A better option would be for the soloist to turn and face the rhythm section so that she can also use eye contact to change chords at the appropriate time.
- *Note: One of the difficult aspects of learning to improvise over chord changes is that, even if the student learns the appropriate chord/scale relationship (or the "declarative knowledge"), the changes move too fast for him to actively cue up that knowledge ("procedural knowledge"). The teacher should use this activity as a way to let the students explore certain chord/scale functions (such as G Dorian or F Mixolydian) in a prolonged setting.*

Assessment

Formative

- The teacher can engage students in discussion on melodic ideas that they developed by having extended time to play chord changes.
- Students can experiment with creating their own short chord/scale progressions to share with classmates.

Summative

- On the basis of the experience students have accumulated in this activity, the teacher can prompt students to compose their own one-chorus solo over a tune's chord changes. The teacher assesses whether students' choruses align with the changes.
- The teacher can prompt students to learn and analyze a master's jazz solo on a modal song. Obviously, if the student transcribes the solo themselves, then that activity is infinitely more valuable, but K–12 students' abilities vary and time may be an obstructing factor. A notated transcription (e.g., from a published transcription book or an online PDF) might be more realistic with scheduling. The teacher assesses students' written ability to identify chord changes and appropriate scales to fit the harmonies.
- The teacher can prompt students to submit an organized written explanation of modal harmony and the accompanying chord/scale relationships for a particular piece in the ensemble's repertoire. The teacher assesses students' ability to identify chord changes and appropriate scales to fit the harmonies.

Lesson Benefits

- Students can practice demonstrating their understanding of the harmonic form by exploring chord/scale relationships without stressful concern for keeping pace with real-time chord changes or monitoring the form of the song.
- Students can apply their aural skills to participate in a jazz harmony improvisation activity.

Recordings

- Artist: Miles Davis
- Album: *Kind of Blue*
- Song: "Flamenco Sketches"
- This activity aside, we cannot recommend this album enough. It is one of the true classics of improvisation and it features many seminal jazz musicians at their finest, including Miles Davis, John Coltrane, Cannonball Adderley, Bill Evans, and Wynton Kelly.

- Artist: John Coltrane
- Album: *My Favorite Things*
- Song: "My Favorite Things"

Beginning Improvisation Ensemble—*Pedal to the Medal*

Description

The purpose of this activity is to engage the students in basic explorative accompaniment over very recognizable melodies. The teacher should present the students with a recognizable melody, ranging from a simple melody such as "Twinkle, Twinkle" to "The Star-Spangled Banner" to a recognizable pop tune from the radio. After the teacher partners students up, one student should play the melody while the other student gives basic pedal-point accompaniments. Reinforcing that dissonance should not be feared and that there are no "wrong notes," the teacher should have the students accompany the melody by ear a different way every time. In this way, students can experience and hear how a melody can be colored in different ways.

Materials

None.

Learning Goals

- The students should develop some experience experimenting with different accompaniment/pedal notes for a simple melody.
- The students should begin to aurally recognize how different melodic intervals sound against certain melody notes.

Procedure

- The teacher should pick a song with a very simple melody. The teacher can (a) pick an easily recognizable song from childhood such as "Twinkle, Twinkle" or "Mary Had a Little Lamb" or, (b) teach a recognizable pop/commercial (the origin does not really matter; it can be from any style) melody to the class; however, this approach will be more time consuming. See Figure 3.14, "Pedal to the Medal" example over "Au Claire de la Lune."
- Once the students can play this melody with relative ease, the teacher should partner up the students. The teacher should ask the first student in each pair to play the melody again and the other student in the pair to play what he perceives to be the *primary* melody note in whole notes or half notes. If the students do not agree on the primary melody note for a given measure or phrase, then the teacher should engage in a conversation with the students in which they eventually agree on a given note. Before moving on to the next step, the teacher should reverse the roles with the paired students.

Sample Accompaniments for "Au Claire de la Lune"

(1) Accompaniment uses only the first note of the song.

(2) Accompaniment uses simple arpeggio notes.

(3) Accompaniment uses a descending major scale starting on the first note of the song.

(4) Random accompaniment notes selected by the student*

* Students, particularly novice students, should not be prompted to utilize sophisticated two-voice counterpoint rules. This activity should encourage broad musical exploration. Some students may arrive at very dissonant accompaniments as is presented in #4. That is simply part of the learning process.

FIGURE 3.14 "Pedal to the Medal" example over "Au Claire de la Lune"

- As the students grow more comfortable with this activity, the "accompaniment" partner in each pair should begin to experiment with different whole- and half-note pedal tones to accompany the melody. *Note: This is a discovery learning activity; this is not prescribed learning. The students should not try to find the "right notes"; they should experiment with notes they like and do not like.*

- *After, and only after, the activity has been performed several times, the teacher can begin to do a post hoc discussion about the students' pedal/accompaniment choices (e.g., "Your E sounded really consonant because it is a major third from the melody note, which is a C").*
- *Advanced*: If one or more students play a harmonic instrument (guitar, piano, keyboard) the teacher can encourage the students to begin with single-note harmonizations. If they grow confident with this process, eventually they can graduate to multi-note harmonizations.

Assessment

Formative

- The teacher can prompt students to describe their chosen accompaniment/pedals and how they sounded. Melody partners give feedback to accompaniment partners as to how the harmonizations felt against the melody.

Summative

- Using a harmonic instrument or music notation program, the students can write an arrangement of a simple melody with an accompaniment/pedal. Students present their harmonized melodies to the class, and the teacher assesses students' ability to describe their harmonization choices. Teachers should be aware that students may describe choices in less technical language: for instance, "I wanted to add a beat to keep the melody going" or "I wanted to hold my note to give the melody a chance to soar."

Lesson Benefits

- Students can creatively experiment with different harmonizations as part of a discovery learning process.
- Students can creatively experiment with different melodic intervals as part of a discovery learning process.

Recordings

Please visit the Oxford University Press Companion Website for an example of a high school general music/modern band program performing this activity. Listening Example 5.1 ▶ is an example of a clarinet and baritone performing the activity. Listening Example 5.2 ▶ is an example of piano and guitar performing the activity.

- Artist: Jim Brickman
- Recording: *Piano Lullabies*

- Artist: Armen Donelian
- Recording: *Grand Ideas, Volume 2: Mystic Heights*

- Artist: Keith Jarrett
- Recording: *The Melody at Night With You*

- Artist: Kenny Werner
- Recording: *Form and Fantasy*
- Song: Check out Werner's versions of Bach's "Sicilienne" and Eric Clapton's "Tears From Heaven."

Intermediate Improvisation Ensemble—*Sonority*

Description

The purpose of this activity is to encourage students to experiment with slowly morphing harmonies. The students are asked to begin with a specific harmony and then gradually transform the harmony through slow interval movement from each of the musicians.

Materials

None.

Learning Goals

- Students will begin to internalize the parts of different harmonies/chords.
- Students will begin to aurally recognize certain harmonies/chords by performing them with their instruments/voices.
- Students will creatively experiment with creating more consonant *and* more dissonant harmonies as a group.

Procedure

- If possible, the teacher should set the class or ensemble up in a circle formation.
- The teacher should give the students a sonority or harmony such as a major or minor triad, an augmented triad, a diminished seventh chord, or a chord built on fourths (the particular harmony choice is not important to the activity and can be chosen according to the repertoire or musical backgrounds of the students).
- The teacher should ask the students to count in order (1, 3, 5, 7, 1, 3, 5, 7, 1, 3, 5, 7 . . .) so that each number is assigned to a part of the chord (root [I], third, fifth, etc.). If students do not have theory or notation background, simply assign them specific pitches (i.e., "Mark, you are going to take the fifth of the C-major triad, so that is G for you.") It is very beneficial for the students if the teacher uses this exercise both as an improvisation activity and as a possible theory teaching device.
- The teacher should first encourage the students to sustain the original sonority so that it is fresh in their ears. The teacher should then encourage the students to slowly move stepwise (half steps or whole steps) away from each student's original note and then slowly work their way back stepwise (half steps or whole steps). It is critical that the students do this very slowly so that they can aurally "absorb" each sonority. Encourage

them to try to move more slowly than their neighbors. *Note: Direction (up or down) is completely up to each student.*

- As the students gain experience with this activity, ask them to experiment with moving toward more consonant and more dissonant harmonies as a group.
- Students who play harmonic instruments (piano, guitar, keyboard) should begin with a single note and eventually move to multiple notes as they gain confidence and experience. If some students already have harmonic movement experience, they can begin with the entire chord outlined by the teacher and engage in gradual harmonic movement.

Assessment

Formative

- The teacher can prompt students to use digital music programs ranging from music notation programs (Sibelius, Finale) to music production programs (GarageBand) and create their own "mood" or "electronica" music track that has slowly shifting harmonies. Peers should pair up and provide positive feedback and suggestions for stretching the harmonies, making them more dissonant or consonant, or finding ways to bring them back to the original chordal structure. The composition checklist (see Figure 3.15) can be used as a guide for student reflection and discussion.

Summative

- The teacher can prompt students to submit an MP3 recording from their formative assessment experience. The teacher assesses the students' compositions on the basis of the composition checklist (see Figure 3.15).

Lesson Benefits

- Students can begin to internalize harmonies more organically through creative performance.
- Students can begin to internalize the possibilities of harmonic movement through improvisation.

_____ Composition begins in a harmonic sonority
_____ Exploration away from the harmonic sonority happens slowly
_____ Dissonance is explored and felt strongest at: _____
_____ Resolution back to the original sonority happens slowly
_____ Dissonance resolves back to the original sonority at: _____
_____ Composition heightens the sonorities and dissonances using other musical elements such as texture and dynamics.

FIGURE 3.15 *Assessment:* Sonority composition checklist

Recordings

- Artist: Miles Davis
- Recording: *In a Silent Way*

- Composer: Richard Wagner
- Work: *Tristan und Isolde*

- Composer: David Julyan
- Work(s): Julyan is a notable film composer who writes many ethereal soundtracks for films, including *Memento, Insomnia*, and *The Descent.*

- Composer: Karlheinz Stockhausen
- Work: *Stimmung*

Rhythm

Beginning Instrumental/Choral Ensemble—*Nontraditional Sounds*

Description

The purpose of this activity is for students to explore their instruments or voices in nontraditional ways. Particularly since many nontraditional sounds are percussive, this activity is ideal for exploring rhythmic improvisation with a younger ensemble. Teachers can encourage students to use their instruments or build or find percussion instruments, or they can easily pull in classroom general music instruments for this lesson.

Materials

(Optional) Homework worksheet on which students can list the nontraditional sounds they explored on their instrument. See Figure 3.16.

Learning Goals

- Students will explore the timbral possibilities of their instruments.
- Students will collectively explore the rhythmic possibilities of their primary instrument and experience group rhythmic improvisation.

Procedure

For part of a homework assignment, have the students take their instruments (if applicable) home and figure out *three* nontraditional sounds (they should record these sounds if at all possible). Examples can include the following:

- Saxophonists popping their keys, trumpeters blowing air through the horn without buzzing, or cellists tapping the wood with their knuckles.

Nontraditional Sounds- Found Sound Collection Journal

Sounds can naturally occur, or they can happen because individuals interact with an object (e.g., spoon stirring in a bowl). Describe your sound, name the object that produced the sound, the setting where it was heard, whether you created the sound using the object, and if you created it, describe the action that made the sound.

Description of Sound	Object	Setting	Created? Y/N	Action that made the sound

FIGURE 3.16 *Assessment:* Nontraditional sounds homework worksheet

- Percussionists can be encouraged to engage in alternate, nontraditional uses for their instruments (e.g., plucking the snares at the bottom of a drum, sliding the bass drum mallet across the skin).
- Choirs are encouraged to use vocal sound effects such as lip smacking, popping, and gasping.
- If the teacher does not wish to have non-instrumental students perform vocal sounds, students can be prompted to bring in one ordinary object from home or nature that makes an interesting "found sound." *Note: Some primary and secondary general music teachers prompt students to "Build Their Own Instrument"*

as part of a project. This approach can certainly feed into the process of such an assignment.

Note: Although certainly not absolutely necessary, the homework approach is encouraged. Using class time for students to figure out sounds can easily result in a chaotic classroom management environment.

- The teacher should begin by demonstrating some nontraditional sound improvisation on his or her instrument or voice. The teacher can then expand by picking two or three eager students and improvising in this manner with them. Eventually the process can be expanded to the entire ensemble.
- If the process is too open ended for the class, there are a number of ways that one can attach more structure to it.
  - Divide the ensemble into groups. A key advantage of this approach is that it requires the students to listen and react. For a logical next step, the teacher can "cue" one or more of the sections at the same time, much like the Texture and Timbre activity, "Gesticulation."
  - Borrow from the next lesson in this section, "Cheap Trick": Select a difficult rhythm from the group's concert repertoire and use that rhythm as the basis for the nontraditional sound improvisation.

Assessment

Formative

- The teacher prompts students to record three nontraditional sounds for homework with their instruments or voices. Sounds are uploaded to a class website. The teacher reviews recordings to evaluate students' breadth and depth of exploration with timbre, tone, and articulation as they find their own rhythms. The teacher also uses the recordings to plan for the upcoming class and give feedback to the group on the scope of their explorations.
- Students listen to peer groups improvise on nontraditional sounds, and provide feedback on the improvisation techniques students are using with their nontraditional sounds.

Summative

- Sometimes changing the context of something that students perceive to be difficult can change their performance on a task. The teacher adopts this approach and asks students to choose a nontraditional sound to perform a difficult rhythm from their concert repertoire. Students record themselves performing the rhythm and describing how they think the nontraditional sound aided in their performance accuracy. For instance, students might comment that the short articulation of a sound made a rhythm easier to perform, or that it was easier to perform a rhythm when they did not have to coordinate difficult tonguing with it. The teacher assesses students' performance on the task and their reasoning on using the nontraditional sound.

Lesson Benefits

- Students can creatively explore the nontraditional possibilities of their instruments (a path that was explored by avant-garde jazz artists such as Cecil Taylor, Alice Coltrane, Albert Ayler, and Lester Bowie, just to name a few).
- Students can also focus completely on rhythm without having to worry about notes.
- Students can all explore improvisation on a roughly equal playing field. It is likely that none of them will have extensive experience with nontraditional sounds.

Recordings

(Note: It would be very messy to try to cover all of the instruments that practice nontraditional sounds in terms of recordings. Therefore, this section will list one or two artists on several instruments/voices).

- Voice: Bobby McFerrin, The Element Choir
- Violin: Mark O'Connor, Zach Brock
- Cello: Matt Turner, Okkyung Lee
- Bass: Avishai Cohen (upright), Victor Wooten (electric)
- Flute: Rahsaan Roland Kirk, Jamie Baum
- Clarinet: Don Byron
- Saxophone: James Carter, Pharoah Sanders, Joseph Jarman
- Trumpet: Lester Bowie, Steven Bernstein, Dave Douglas
- Trombone: Ed Neumeister, Roswell Rudd, Jeffrey Albert
- Euphonium/tuba: Bob Stewart
- Piano: Cecil Taylor, Myra Melford
- Guitar: Derek Bailey, Bill Frisell, Pat Metheny
- Drums: Matt Wilson, Ed Blackwell, Tyshawn Sorey
- Mallet percussion: Gary Burton, Kevin Norton, Peyton MacDonald

Intermediate Instrumental/Choral Ensemble—*Cheap Trick*

Description

The purpose of this lesson is to use group free improvisation to support students' performance and understanding of challenging rhythms. In particular, this activity can be used to place a difficult rhythm in a different, more explorative musical context. Students will use a difficult rhythm (such as a rhythm that the students struggle with in the concert repertoire) as a rhythmic motif for a large ensemble free improvisation.

Materials
A visible example of a pentatonic scale, either printed for the students or drawn on the board.

Learning Goals
- Students will gain greater control and awareness over the difficult rhythm in question.
- Students will gain conceptual rhythmic awareness, particularly with regard to the rhythm in question.
- Students will explore open-ended textural improvisations by using rhythmic motives as prompts.

Procedure
- The teacher should select a difficult rhythm from a band/orchestra/choir piece.
- The teacher should aurally model the rhythm for the students with him or her playing it first, then having the group play it back as an ensemble.
- When the teacher feels that the students are ready, he should present the students with a pentatonic scale (preferably in the same key as the piece with the difficult rhythm, modulations/key changes not withstanding) written on the board or printed up. The teacher should then select two to three students and instruct them to improvise with her, but using only the selected rhythm and the notes of the pentatonic scale. To help students feel comfortable, we recommend that players perform the rhythm at the same tempo. At first, it may seem like a harmonic exercise with players performing the rhythm on different pentatonic tones. As students become comfortable and more accurate with the rhythm, they may perform the rhythm at different tempos. This exercise can be done in this stage of the lesson, or later, as the whole ensemble demonstrates their performance accuracy with the rhythm.
- If the students still seem apprehensive, the teacher can repeat this process with different groups of two to three students until the teacher believes that the students are ready to take on this activity as a larger ensemble.
- When the students are ready to perform this activity as a larger ensemble, this type of large-scale textural exercise can easily become a cacophony. There are a few ways the teacher can address this problem:
  - Encourage the students to listen and leave space. Many novice improvisers automatically assume that they must play all the time when they improvise. Encourage the students to put down their instruments (or voices!) two-thirds of the time and encourage them to listen for musical "openings" or "entry points." Pat Harbison (Indiana University professor and jazz trumpet virtuoso)

uses the excellent analogy of painting with colors. If you play too many notes with no contrast (especially as a group) it is like adding too many colors to the canvas, an approach that inevitably produces black (and a lack of variety) every time.

- o Direct some musical prompts. Examples include the following:
  - Have different groups of students play different dynamics or articulations.
  - Have some students play the rhythm at a fast tempo, while others simultaneously play it at a slow tempo.
  - *Note: If the teacher is particularly concerned about the activity becoming overwhelming in a large ensemble, the activity can be done with a smaller sectional or lesson groups.*
  - Students can be encouraged to combine this exercise with the "Nontraditional Sounds" activity (without the pentatonic scale structure).
  - *Advanced:* Students can partake in the same activity except apply elements of augmentation or diminution in the same manner as "Brahmsian Improvisation" in Section III, "Melody."

Assessment

Formative

- The teacher asks the students to suggest musical prompts or organizational ideas for the activity. The teacher and students together informally assess the performance based on their organizational ideas. The teacher uses students' comments and performance to adapt future practice.
- The teacher prompts students to record the activity in groups of four. The teacher provides feedback on the performance and manipulations of the rhythm.

Summative

- The teacher demonstrates how some of the rhythmic manipulations would appear in notation (using the pentatonic scale) and asks students to compose at home a short piece based on the selected rhythm. The teacher can then assess the composition by using the checklist, from the lesson on "Brahmsian Improvisation" in "Melody." The teacher can choose to add or replace the existing checklist categories with new musical categories such as the translation of the rhythm into other time signatures, and/or how it appears with different dynamics, ranges, articulations, and tempos.

Lesson Benefits

- Students will engage in creative rhythmic exploration while clarifying conceptual understanding of a difficult rhythm (it does not matter whether the rhythm is either part of concert repertoire or simply a way the teacher wishes to expand the students' rhythmic learning). This exploration, in turn, can enhance other outcome skills, such as sight-reading.

- For growing musicians to understand a "concept" instead of an isolated motor skill, they must grasp a fuller spectrum of the idea, in this case a single rhythm. One way to promote conceptual rhythmic learning is to have the students perform the rhythm in a variety of contexts, such as different tempos, and note groupings.
- Music teachers often model difficult rhythms for students through their instrument/singing/tapping, a *highly* effective strategy that we have used in countless instances. However, having students explore one rhythm in a variety of ways allows them to cement their own understanding of the rhythm, and allows them to identify when and how they perform the rhythm best.

Recordings

Please visit the Oxford University Press Companion Website Listening Example 6.1 ⊙ *for an example of an elementary school concert band performing this activity.*

- Artist: Miles Okazaki
- Recording: *Mirror*

- Artist: Bela Fleck, Zakir Hussein, and Edgar Meyer with the Detroit Symphony Orchestra
- Recording: *The Melody of Rhythm*

- Artist: Thelonious Monk
- Recording: *Brilliant Corners*
- Song: "Brilliant Corners"

- Artist: Fred Frith
- Recording: *Gravity*

- Artist: Joe Lovano
- Recording: *Quartets: Live at the Village Vanguard*
- Song: "Fort Worth"

Beginning Jazz Ensemble—*Swingology*

Description

Along with improvisation, *swing* is one of the key novel concepts presented to most beginning jazz ensembles. Although there is certainly a fair share of jazz arrangements that make use of straight eighth notes as part of rock and funk rhythms, the crux of the large ensemble tradition is grounded in swing, a concept that must be mastered for any exemplary jazz ensemble. This activity attempts to streamline conceptual rhythmic learning with group improvisation. It is likely that both of these concepts will be new to the majority of beginning jazz students. For better understanding, a step-by-step process that gradually increases in conceptual adventurousness is presented.

Materials

- "Jazz Rhythm Syllabus," from the "Blues" lesson in "Harmony."
- For this activity, we highly recommend that the teacher play some of the recommended recordings for the students. Traditionally, jazz is an aurally transmitted art form. Therefore, teachers are encouraged to keep the discussion focused on actual sounds, feel, and groove in their favorite examples.

Learning Goals

- Students will begin to develop a contextual awareness of commonly used jazz swing rhythms.
- Students will begin to explore a more rhythmic (as opposed to harmonic or melodic) approach to improvising.

Procedure

- The teacher should examine Figure 3.12, "Jazz Rhythm Syllabus" (reprised from the "Blues" lesson in "Harmony") and select two or three rhythms from the document.
- The teacher can certainly hand out the Syllabus to the students but should first work on the concept aurally with the students by modeling the rhythms for each of the sections.
- The rhythm section should vamp on a single chord. It would be wise for the teacher to ask for a simple medium-tempo shuffle groove. As the ensemble gains more experience with the activity, the teacher and students can begin to experiment with other grooves. *Note: Although the rhythm section should certainly be included in this activity the dilemma is that it is necessary that they provide the harmonic and rhythmic accompaniment for the activity.*
  - *If there is more than one player for each instrument (piano, bass, drums, guitar) then there is an easy solution. The two students on the same instrument can alternate between participating in the activity (they can join any one of the wind sections) and providing the rhythm part.*
  - *If there is **not** more than one player for each instrument, we recommend the following approaches:*
    - *Piano and guitar players can play section rhythms with their chord comping.*
    - *If there is only one bassist and/or drummer, the teacher should encourage each player to alternate between playing the accompaniment and joining other sections with "Jazz Rhythm Syllabus" rhythms (Figure 3.12).*
- The students can first explore the activity with no improvisation just to get a sense of the process. More specifically, the teacher can prompt the entire jazz ensemble to repeat one of the "Jazz Rhythm Syllabus" rhythms until they can perform it with relative ease. *Note: Most of the students will not know how to harmonically or melodically structure the chosen rhythm. We recommend that the teacher begin by having the students perform the rhythms with the root note of the vamped chord to simplify the process.*

- After the students have performed a few of the "Jazz Rhythm Syllabus" rhythms as written, the teacher can start encouraging some student agency by having the members of a section determine their own rhythmic choice from the Syllabus.
- After the students have picked their own rhythms several times, the teacher can either ask for section volunteers or ask a member of the section to come up with a variation on the rhythm that the section just played. After coming up with the variation, the rest of the section should play this variation in unison as well.
- The next step is to have a member of each section improvise different variations over the section rhythm in time. Depending on the situation, the teacher can have one student do this at a time if the teacher wants to clearly discern the variations or have several section "improvisers" do it at the same time if the safety of group improvisation is desired.
- As students begin to gain facility and confidence in this activity, the teacher can begin to move students to play the rhythms with notes other than the root of the vamped chord. Review Figure 3.13 from the "Blues" lesson for an example. The following progression would be practical:
  ○ Students perform the rhythm or variations on a single part of the vamped chord, such as the third, fifth, seventh, or ninth *Note: This can be a great way for the teacher to work on jazz theory.*
  ○ Students perform the rhythm or variations on two notes from the vamped chord. The teacher can model the exact contour of the pattern.
  ○ Students perform the rhythm or variations on a simple blues scale or pentatonic figure (depending on the vamped chord). The teacher will probably have to demonstrate a model example so that the students can perform it as a section or ensemble.
  ○ Students perform the rhythm or variations by using a given scale based on the vamped chord. Once again, the teacher will probably have to demonstrate a model example so that the students can perform it as a section or ensemble.
- The final step is to have individual students solo over these concurrent rhythms as if they were background riffs in a big band arrangement. More specifically, the soloist would thematically develop a particular selected rhythm. Masters of this approach in jazz would include (but are not limited to) Louis Armstrong, Lester Young, Harry "Sweets" Edison, Clark Terry, Ray Brown, Bobby Timmons, Les McCann, Count Basie, Al Grey, and Paul Gonsalves.

Assessment

Formative

- The teacher provides students with recording recommendations to illustrate exemplary models of swing. Students create a "Riff Journal" and are encouraged to enter riffs from great recordings (i.e., Count Basie, Benny Goodman) as well as riffs created in jazz band rehearsals. The teacher reviews journals and adapts practice as necessary.

- The teacher listens to student-created variations on the swing rhythms, and provides immediate feedback on the students' ideas and the performance of their rhythms.

Summative

- Teacher asks students to get in small groups including at least one rhythm section player. Students select three to four swing rhythms from the chart to play and record with rhythm-player accompaniment. The group performance is recorded. The teacher assesses students' swing performance on their selected rhythms.

Lesson Benefits

- The lessons embraces student-centered differentiation (students can improvise according to their comfort levels).
- Students can play jazz swing rhythms and articulations in a low-pressure, fun environment.
- Students can explore a more rhythmic approach to improvisation.

Recordings

- Artist: Harry "Sweets" Edison [Trumpet]
- Recording: *Ben & Sweets*
- Song: "Better Go"

- Artist: Duke Ellington (*Note: This recording has infinite value for this lesson, as both the Ellington arrangement and the almost riot-inducing Paul Gonsalves tenor solo both exemplify this type of rhythmic variation*)
- Recording: *Ellington at Newport*
- Song: "Diminuendo and Crescendo in Blue"

- Artist: Benny Goodman
- Recording: *Live at Carnegie Hall*
- Song: "Sing, Sing, Sing"

- Artist: Count Basie
- Recording: (This song can be found on any number of Basie "Collection" Recordings)
- Song: "Jumping at the Woodside"

Intermediate Jazz Ensemble—*Synchronicity*

Description

This activity presents the same concept as "Swingology" except it is used over the complete form of a tune.

Materials

- "Jazz Fragment Supplement," Figure 3.17.

FIGURE 3.17 Jazz Fragment Supplement

- For this activity, we highly recommend that the teacher play some of the recommended recordings for the students. Traditionally, jazz is an aurally transmitted art form. Therefore, keep discussion focused on actual sounds, feel, and groove in your favorite examples.

Learning Goals
- Students will begin to develop a contextual awareness of commonly used jazz swing rhythms.
- Students will begin to explore a more rhythmic (as opposed to harmonic or melodic) approach to improvising.
- Students will begin to explore how different rhythms fit into different harmonic contexts.

Procedure

- This activity should be performed like "Swingology" except, instead of the ensemble's vamping over a single chord, the activity should be extended to tune forms such as the 12-bar blues, rhythm changes, or any other set of chord progressions. More specifically, the teacher and students should transpose a given rhythmic and melodic "fragment" over the chord changes of a given tune (see Figure 3.17, "Jazz Fragment Supplement").

- For this activity, the teacher and students are encouraged to use the "Jazz Fragment Supplement" for specific rhythmic examples with the chord changes for a particular tune (it can easily be a tune from the ensemble's repertoire). The "Jazz Fragment Supplement" is preferable to the "Jazz Rhythm Syllabus" for this activity because single measure-long rhythms can be used more flexibly for a complete harmonic progression (as opposed to a vamping chord). The ultimate goal is for individual student soloists to use a specific rhythm throughout their entire solos. Consider the following:

  o The students can first explore the activity with no improvisation just to get a sense of the process. More specifically, the teacher can prompt the entire jazz ensemble to repeat one of the "Jazz Fragment Supplement" rhythms in unison until they can perform it with relative ease. Most of the students will not know how to harmonically or melodically structure the chosen rhythm. We recommend that the teacher model a rhythm and begin by having the students perform the rhythms with the root note of the chord changes to simplify the process.

  o As students begin to gain facility and confidence over this activity, the teacher can begin to move students to play the rhythms with notes other than the root of the chord changes.

    ▪ Students perform the rhythm or variations on a single part of the vamped chord, such as the third, fifth, seventh, or ninth (this can be a great way for the teacher to work on jazz theory).

    ▪ Students perform the rhythm or variations on two notes from the chord changes. *The teacher can model the exact contour of the pattern.*

    ▪ Students perform the rhythm or variations by using a given scale based on the chord changes. Once again, the teacher will probably have to demonstrate a model example so that the students can perform it as a section or ensemble.

- After the students gain experience with several set examples, eager students should come up with their own rhythmic/melodic "fragments." To facilitate this activity, the teacher can either (a) have each student choose a rhythm from the "Jazz Fragment Supplement" and ask the student to come up with a melodic contour for the fragment or (b) have the student come up with his or her own rhythm and then present that student an idea for the fragment's melodic contour. The ensemble should then be prompted to transpose the student's motif over a tune's chord changes.

- As with "Swingology," the final step is to have individual students thematically develop a given rhythm as part of an individual solo.

- When the teacher or the students feel ready, individual students can perform this activity over a given set of chord changes. Remember that this is a *process-over-product* activity. Artist-level jazz improvisers do not typically solo in this way on an extended basis. Instead, students should think of it as a way to improve their improvisational skills through a specific practice approach.
- If the student soloist is nervous or apprehensive, he can simply play the selected rhythm on the same exact beat every two or four measures (while trying to fit the rhythm to the harmonic chord changes). When the student becomes more comfortable with this approach, he can experiment with placing the rhythm in different measures, on different beats, and on different parts of the beat.
- *Advanced:* An ambitious student can try to organically weave in and out of a rhythmic motif as the masters in the *Recordings* section demonstrate.

Assessment

Formative

- The teacher provides students with recording recommendations to illustrate exemplary models of swing. Students create a "Riff Journal" and are encouraged to enter riffs from great recordings (i.e., Count Basie, Benny Goodman) as well as riffs created in jazz band rehearsals. The teacher reviews journals and adapts practice as necessary.
- The teacher listens to students swing a rhythm over the form of a song or twelve-bar blues and provides immediate feedback on students' performances. The "Synchronicity" rubric (see Figure 3.18) is used as a tool for discussion on students' performances. The points of discussion may include whether the swing rhythm was played with a proper duration and feel, if articulations and accents were consistent with the rhythmic swing, if the tempo was maintained, and whether the form was followed.

Summative

- The teacher records students taking turns performing the swing rhythm over the form with rhythm section accompaniment. The teacher assesses students' swing performance over the form by using the "Synchronicity" rubric (see Figure 3.18). However, it should be noted that before a teacher uses the rubric as a summative assessment, students should have a clear understanding of the harmonic functions within the form and be able to play through them without inhibiting their rhythmic performance.

Lesson Benefits

- This lesson allows the students to repeatedly perform and explore the conceptual nuance of rhythms, this time in the context of tune forms and chord changes.
- The lesson allows students to engage in structural awareness of tunes and chord changes.

	3	2	1
Rhythms demonstrate proper duration and swing feel/ (For Rhythm Section) Accompaniment is performed with appropriate "pocket" and swing feel.	Rhythms *always* demonstrate proper duration and swing feel/(For Rhythm Section) Accompaniment is *consistently* performed with appropriate "pocket" and swing feel.	Rhythms *mostly* demonstrate proper duration and swing feel/(For Rhythm Section) Accompaniment is *mostly* performed with appropriate "pocket" and swing feel.	Rhythms *rarely* or *never* demonstrate proper duration and swing feel/(For Rhythm Section) Accompaniment is *rarely or never* performed with appropriate "pocket" and swing feel.
Articulations and accents are consistent with rhythmic swing feel.	Articulations and accents are *always* performed in conjunction with rhythmic swing feel.	Articulations and accents are *mostly* performed in conjunction with rhythmic swing feel.	Articulations and accents are *rarely or never performed* in conjunction with rhythmic swing feel.
Maintains tempo.	The tempo is maintained throughout the form.	The tempo changes 1-2 times throughout the form.	The tempo changes more than two times throughout the form.
Follows harmonic form.	The changes in the harmonic form are always followed.	The changes in the harmonic form are sometimes followed but there are 1-2 inaccuracies.	The changes in the harmonic form are not followed on more than 2 occasions.

FIGURE 3.18 *Assessment:* "Synchronicity" rubric

- The lesson allows students to explore rhythmic motives as a means for soloing over chord changes.
- The lesson allows differentiated learning by letting students proceed at their own pace. Students have the choice of playing a set rhythm with their section, inventing a variation on a rhythm, or participating in a full group improvisation.

Recordings
- Artist: Harry "Sweets" Edison [trumpet]
- Recording: *Ben & Sweets*
- Song: "Better Go"

- Artist: Lionel Hampton and his Orchestra (soloist: Illinois Jacquet [tenor saxophone])
- Recording: *Flyin' Home: The Best of the Verve Years*
- Song: "Flyin' Home"

- Artist: Dave Brubeck (soloist: Paul Desmond)
- Recording: *Jazz at Oberlin*
- Song: "Perdido"

Beginning Improvisation Ensemble—*Rhythmic Mash-Up*

Description

The purpose of this activity is to use melody fragments from common tunes or pop songs to imitate the unique textural combinations found in mash-ups (a recording or performance that consists of a mix of two or more songs).

Materials

Recordings of different pop melodies. The teacher can also choose to notate each of the melodies for the students (this task is very easy to accomplish with music notation programs such as Finale, Sibelius, and Noteflight) but, while more expeditious for the students, ready-made notations will not develop students' abilities to play by ear and transpose as well.

Learning Goals

- The students will be able to integrate rhythms and melodies as part of a larger texture.
- The teacher and students will integrate difficult and sometimes dissimilar rhythmic and melodic fragments.
- The students will eventually be able to transpose melodies into different keys.

Procedure

- For this approach, the teacher should break the class into two groups. The teacher should then have the two groups go into two different spaces where they cannot hear one another (for example, one group might stay in the classroom and one might go out in the hallway, if appropriate). The students should take instruments with them, if possible.
- The teacher should instruct each group to select a pop song (or any accessible song) and to learn it, either through singing or on their instruments or both. If needed, a digital medium such as a digital tablet can be used by each group to learn the song.
  - One group should not be aware of the other group's song choice.
  - The teacher should direct *both* groups to learn the song in an easy key such as C or F, regardless of the original key of the recorded version. Some beginner groups may need help finding the starting pitch of their pop songs if they do not begin on the tonic.
  - After both groups have learned their respective songs in the chosen key, the teacher should bring both groups back together to perform at the same time. The teacher should challenge the groups to combine both songs into a coherent arrangement or *mash-up*. Students will need to reconcile the different tempos and rhythms of the two songs. Mash-ups often create interesting interlocking rhythms or shifts in meter, but the students need to discover these possibilities. After the performance, the groups can discuss what fit well and how they might improve upon it. Students should then try performing together for a second time.

Assessment

Formative

- Students can come up with their own collection of melodies that they have learned by ear from recordings. The students should also be encouraged to try their hand at transposing all of the melodies into a single key and teaching the melodic fragments to the other students in the class. With younger students, we encourage teachers to do this with simple well-known folk or pop tunes. Students partner together, and peers provide feedback to one another on the writing of the fragments, and then partners try to play different fragments at the same time.
- The teacher prompts students to form small groups and video record their own live versions of this activity. Student groups share recordings with other groups, and groups comment on one another's performances—particularly the relationship between the student arranger/conductor and the sounds created by the ensemble. *Note: Students should be discouraged from posting copyrighted music on public video forums such as YouTube or Facebook. Instead, consider using a forum like Vialogues that allow students to make timestamped comments on uploaded videos for private viewing.*

Summative

- The teacher asks students to write a reflection or paper on a specific mash-up recording. The teacher assesses a student's ability to translate ideas discussed and performed in class to her analysis of the mash-up.
- If students have the requisite software experience, the teacher can ask students to create their own mash-ups with a program such as Garageband or Audacity. Before the mashups are assessed, the teacher and students can decide on a grading framework that relates to their experiences in class. For instance, the class could consider the following questions to design an assessment: Did the mashup keep a pulse? How did the mashup merge the two tempos? How did it combine the two different rhythms? Did it have interesting entrances and fade-outs? Did the sound pan widely?

Lesson Benefits

- Students can use recognizable preexisting rhythms and melodies to create new textures.
- Students can experiment with flexibly interweaving song fragments that come from different tempos and rhythms.

Recordings

Please visit the Oxford University Press Companion Website for an example of a high school orchestra performing this activity. Listening Example 7.1 ⊙ features one group's song, Listening Example 7.2 ⊙ features the other group's song, and Listening Example 7.3 ⊙ features the two songs "mashed up" for the activity.

There are several terrific examples of mash-up artists; what is more difficult is screening mash-up recordings for lyrics that are not profane in accordance with the guidelines of a given K–12 school, district, and/or community. Since different schools have different guidelines in this regard, we recommend that teachers choose recordings on the basis of that school or district's guidelines.

- Artists: Girl Talk, DJ Earworm, The Kleptones

- Artist: Charlie Hunter Trio
- Recording: *bing, bing, bing!*
- Song: "Come as You Are" (This is actually a performed quasi-mash-up of two Nirvana songs, "Smells Like Teen Spirit" and "Come as You Are")

Intermediate Improvisation Ensemble—*I Have No Time*

Description

The stated goal of this activity is very simple. The ensemble should attempt to play a group improvisation with no discernable meter. Musicians spend their lives in trying to play in sync in terms of a given meter or tempo, so one might assume that this activity might represent some type of easy child's play. Nothing could be further from the truth. It can be quite challenging to play without a sense of meter and even more challenging to sustain it. However, it can also be quite a liberating and fun challenge for students, particularly if they are playing on electronic instruments.

Materials

Video or audio of background sound phenomena such as waves, construction equipment, traffic, bird calls, or wind.

Learning Goals

- Students will experiment with meter less improvisation.
- Students will explore how other musical components such as melody, harmony, and texture can be utilized without a set meter.
- Students will learn to move from playing in a given meter to playing without a set meter and vice versa.

Procedure

- The goal of this lesson plan is to provide several entry point ideas for meter less improvisation. It is up to the teacher to select entry points on the basis of his discretion and particular group of students.

- *Entry point ideas.* To acclimate students to this process, we suggest students warm up with playing two different folk tunes, similar to "Rhythmic Mash-Up" in different meters at the same time. For example, half of the class can play "Mary Had a Little Lamb" [𝄴] while the other half simultaneously plays "Greensleeves" [𝄳]. As students become more comfortable with this activity, they can begin to stretch the tempo to feel more freedom in their playing. Teachers may want to transpose the folk tunes into the same key to keep the focus on meter less performance and not on harmonic dissonance. After the warm-up the teacher can approach meter less free improvisation performance by using the following entry points:
  - First, have half the students perform an open-ended free improvisation in the first meter while the other half performs in a different typical meter (e.g., have half of the students improvise in 𝄴 while the other half perform in 𝄳 or 𝄵).
  - A second approach is to begin the activity in a designated meter but improvise with different tempos. Have half of the students improvise at one tempo while the other half improvise in the same meter, *but* at a much slower or much faster tempo. When the students have developed some experience with this activity, try dividing the group up into three or four different tempos over the same meter.
  - Select a naturally occurring sonic phenomenon that does not fit into a particular meter. *Note: Examples include waves, construction equipment, traffic, and wind.* Have the students perform a group improvisation that imitates the sonic events of that occurrence. Feel free to play a video or audio recording of that occurrence for the students, if necessary.
- *Advanced Extensions*:
  - Have the students imitate one of the recommended recordings.
  - Have the students begin with no meter and move *from chaos to clarity* by having them eventually morph into a discernable meter or groove.

Assessment

Formative

- The teacher asks students to record a naturally occurring sonic phenomenon that does not fit into an exact meter (ocean waves, a dish washer, car traffic). Students can present ideas on how the class can imitate this phenomenon.
- The teacher prompts students to record themselves performing this activity and can analyze the musical proceedings and offer suggestions as to how the group/class can perform meter less improvisation with greater ease.

Summative

- The teacher asks students to select one of the listed recordings and write a short analysis of the performance. The teacher assesses students' ability to describe the meter-less or metrically flexible setting in terms of musical developments that affect the overall feeling of melody, harmony, and texture.

- If either the teacher or the students wish to expand on this, students can write a more in-depth paper on one or more of the musicians or groups (such as Ornette Coleman or Paul Motian).

Lesson Benefits

- Students can explore metric or tempo flexibility in an improvisation setting.
- Improvisation in a meter less setting can give students conceptual tools for improvising in a meter or tempo with great flexibility.

Recordings

- Artist: Bill Frisell
- Recording: *Ghost Town*
- Song: "What a World, Under a Golden Sky, Winter Always Turns to Spring"

- Artist: Paul Motian Trio
- Recording: *I Have the Room Above Her*

- Artist: Ornette Coleman/Joaquim Kühn
- Recording: *Colors: Live from Leipzig*

- Artist: John Abercrombie
- Recording: *Gateway*
- Song: "Sorcery No. 1"

- Artist: Branford Marsalis
- Recording: *Requiem*
- Song: "Lykief"

- Artist: Keith Jarrett Quartet
- Recording: *Byablue*
- Song: "Trieste"

Texture and Timbre

Beginning Instrumental/Choral Ensemble—*Indie "In D"*

Description

The purpose of this activity is to approach textural improvisation with the mindset of minimalist composition. More specifically, this activity builds off Terry Riley's famous composition, *In C*. The lesson takes the basic concept of *In C*, which allows the musicians to perform a series of composed melodic fragments (a) starting whenever each musician prefers, and (b) repeating each fragment as many times as each musician prefers. In this lesson, the concept gives the students the opportunity to improvise in a low-pressure setting with very little variability. Each student does not spontaneously improvise the melodic fragments but, instead, has the agency to determine when to begin and how many times to play each fragment.

Materials

Sheet music with a list of short musical phrases, all in identical numbered format. All necessary transpositions should be made available according to the specific ensemble, and non-pitched percussion parts should include only rhythms and articulations (sustained notes can be performed with rests or rolls). Figure 3.19 can be used as an example.

Learning Goals

- Students will explore texture through the improvised pacing of specific melodic fragments.
- Students will explore spontaneous creativity through an individualized approach to the pacing and range on the basis of prescribed melodic fragments.
- Students will learn to creatively explore texture as a single "ensemble unit."

FIGURE 3.19 "Indie in D" fragment chart

Procedure

- The teacher can either use the provided fragment chart (see Figure 3.19) or on his or her own create one based on concert repertoire. A teacher can easily do so by coming up with or borrowing fragments from various sources and simply transposing them into the key of D major (or any other key; D is simply used for the title). The important element is that all the student musicians should have their fragments in the same concert key to give tonal order to the texture.
- Unlike some of the other activities in this book, musicians are expected to play the notation exactly as written in numerical order; *however,* they can repeat each fragment as many times as they wish and, thus, the piece ends when the last musician is finished repeating the last fragment.
- The number of fragments is entirely up to the teacher and can be constructed to fit the time management needs of the teaching period. However, too few (i.e., two to three)

fragments will not give the students a chance to adequately explore the activity and too many fragments might bore the students.

- To give an idea of how many fragments should be used, Terry Riley's *In C* consists of 53 fragments and typically takes from 45 to 90 minutes to perform. Needless to say, this time frame is almost certainly too long for a school ensemble, so teachers should plan accordingly.
- If the teacher wishes to challenge the students further, she can transpose the activity into a more difficult key or encourage the students to vary the range/register or dynamics of each of the fragments.

Assessment

Formative

- The teacher and students engage in reflective dialogue on a layered performance of fragments. Group questions might include the following: How did we perform creatively as an ensemble? How effectively did we perform as a single unit? The teacher can adapt the activity either by creating a new fragment or by challenging students to meet new musical goals with the use of the existing chart.

Summative

- Students perform their chart a second time, and the teacher records it. Students can either write a reflection in class or online addressing the following: How did I perform creatively as an individual? How did I perform this activity differently from last time? The teacher assesses the depth of response as well as students' ability to self-assess changes in their performances.

Lesson Benefits

- Students explore different textures with same basic melodic material.
- Students can explore group improvisation within the safe constraints of predetermined melodic material.
- Students can safely explore improvisation through variation in pacing, dynamics, and register/range.
- Students can practice playing/singing in different keys.
- Students can practice reading and playing/singing different articulations.
- Students can practice playing/singing different rhythms.

Recordings

Please visit the Oxford University Press Companion Website for Listening Example 8.1 ▶ *of an elementary band performing this activity.*

- Any recording of Terry Riley's composition, *In C* (the music teacher is encouraged to check out different recordings as each version *will* sound different).

- Composer: Steve Reich
- Piece: *Music for Pieces of Wood*

- Artists: Gary Burton/Chick Corea Duo
- Recording: *Crystal Silence*

- Artist: Aaron Parks Quartet
- Recording: *Invisible Cinema*

- Artist: The Who
- Recording: *Who's Next*
- Song: "Baba O'Riley" (named after Terry Riley) and "Won't Get Fooled Again"

Intermediate Instrumental/Choral Ensemble—*Braxtonian March*

Description

The purpose of this activity is to apply some variability and basic textural improvisation to the genre of marches, particularly those epitomized by John Philip Sousa. This lesson is loosely influenced by some of the improvisational concepts used by composer/improviser Anthony Braxton in his march, *22-M, Opus 58*. *Note: We realize that marches are a mainstay of many ensemble curriculums and typically are not changed during rehearsal. However, the goal of this activity is to get students to engage with the textural details of the selected march in a process-over-product activity.*

Materials

The teacher has the option of using a written march.

Note: Although marches are much more common for concert band, chorus and orchestra ensembles are also encouraged to take advantage of this activity. Other examples might include overtures for orchestra, and oratorios for choir. The idea is to explore texture in a way that reveals musical form.

Learning Goals

- Students will creatively experiment with textures by using the culturally recognizable template/style of the march genre.
- Students will creatively experiment with textures by using notated marches.
- Students will creatively experiment with melodic/rhythmic ornamentation by using notated marches.
- Students will explore textural roles that differ from those typically found for certain instruments (i.e., flutes play bassline instead of low brass playing the line).

Procedure

- The purpose of this activity is to use the cultural format of the march (in any style, whether it be Sousa or a funeral dirge) as a template for textural improvisation.
- The extent or the adventurousness of this activity can run the gamut and is entirely up to the discretion of the music teacher. More specifically, it may benefit the music teacher to start the class with a more conservative format for this activity (slight ornamentation on a notated concert repertoire) and gradually progress toward a more adventurous format (one more akin to Anthony Braxton's avant-garde marches).
- With this activity, a chronological plan is less important than awareness of the various options available to the teacher and the ensemble.
  - A list of these options includes the following:
    - Giving the students the freedom to alter rhythms slightly (i.e., turn two quarter notes into a dotted quarter note and an eighth note.
    - Insert grace notes or neighbor tones into the original melody.
    - Change staccato articulations into legato articulations and vice versa.
    - Change loud dynamics into soft dynamics and vice versa.
    - An approach more akin to Braxton's composition on *22-M, Opus 58* (from the recording *Creative Orchestra Music 1976*), in which a notated march is performed as written but various "vamps" are inserted where students (individuals or groups) can then improvise (see Figure 3.20 for an excerpt taken from Sousa's "The Washington Post" that would serve as a useful vamp setting). *Note: It may behoove the teacher to try this approach with a smaller group of students (e.g., a sectional group).* Examples of vamps can include isolated versions or any combination of the following:
      - A characteristic "oom-pah" bass part as played by the low brass section (this activity often involves musicians playing the I and V of a chord on beats one and three). Teachers can demonstrate how students can play this in the concert key of the piece.
      - Having students improvise (harmonically free) over the percussion part for a given notated march.
      - Various combinations of instruments playing the "trio" section of the march while others improvise.

The teacher may help cue the entrances of the notated parts and provide a cue for improvised parts. The teacher should also provide direction as to when to return to the score. Some students may want to improvise as individuals, an option that is, of course, perfectly fine. If the students are apprehensive, the teacher should encourage them to perform in groups. A benefit of the upbeat nature of many marches is that students can be encouraged to play cacophonously or with nontraditional sounds, an approach that often produces humorous results.

"The Washington Post" March Excerpt

John Philip Sousa

FIGURE 3.20 Sample vamp material using "The Washington Post" march excerpt

Advanced and adventurous ensembles. These ensembles can experiment with trading up "traditional march roles." For example, the teacher can have the higher timbre flutes or violins take on a traditional low brass "oom-pah" part. Another option is having the tonal instruments play a percussion part while having the percussion instruments play a march melody.

Assessment

Formative

- The teacher asks students to reflect on the choices of a particular version of this activity. The teacher listens and provides additional feedback to stretch students' understandings of texture and melodic/rhythmic ornamentation.

Summative

- The teacher prompts students to sketch out a formal analysis of the selected march for this activity. The teacher assesses students' ability to recognize the textures that exist across the ensemble at given points in the score.

Lesson Benefits

- Students explore improvisation within the context of a familiar cultural style (the march).
- Students can creatively explore texture in the familiar context of a march.
- Students can explore creative textures and nontraditional sounds in a safe ensemble environment.
- The teacher can use this activity as an opportunity for students to learn historical examples of marches.

Recordings

- Artist: Anthony Braxton
- Recording: *Creative Orchestra Music 1976*
- Piece: *22-M, Opus 58*

- Composer: Charles Ives
- Piece: *Three Places in New England* (All three movements are encouraged but "Putnam's Camp" is particularly interesting, as it is meant to evoke two different marching bands marching *toward each other*.

- Composer: John Philip Sousa
- Pieces: Any of his excellent American marches such as "The Stars and Stripes Forever!," "The Washington Post," "The Thunderer," or "The Liberty Bell."

- Composer: Hector Berlioz
- Piece: *Symphonie fantastique*, fourth movement: "March au supplice" (March to the Scaffold)

- Composer: Igor Stravinsky
- Piece: *In memoriam Dylan Thomas: Dirge Canons and Song for Tenor, String Quartet, and Four Trombones*

Beginning Jazz Ensemble—*Instigation Sounds*

Description

One approach to engaging students in interesting textural improvisation is to use a strategy suggested by trombonist and scholar Jeff Albert called "instigation roles." More specifically, this approach involves breaking down a jazz ensemble into three or four groups of students and assigning different "musical roles" to them. The general concept is that the specificity of a given role (e.g., pointy, octaves, low notes) prompts or "instigates" the students toward musical explorations that they might not have experienced had they taken a more "blank slate" approach.

Materials

None.

Learning Goals

- Students will develop experience improvising within the framework of a very particular musical quality.
- Students will explore the spectrum of possibilities for a given instigation sound or musical quality.

Procedure

- The teacher should break the jazz ensemble into three or four groups of students and assign different "musical roles" to them. To begin the activity, the teacher should have each student take a number from 1 to 4 (they can count off 1, 2, 3, 4, 1, 2, 3, 4, etc.). Then the teacher assigns musical roles for each of the groups. For example, the musical role for group 1 might be to perform long tones. The musical role for group 2 might be to perform a repeating rhythmic figure. The musical role for group 3 can be staccato quarter notes, and the role for group 4 can be fragmented, melodic flourishes (some of these might require a demonstration from the teacher).
- The director should then signal each group to enter as each group layers on top of one another. Although the time between group entrances may vary, 10 to 20 seconds between group entrances is appropriate. The director should be sure to tell the students that there are no right or wrong notes, harmonies, rhythms, or contours. The director should also tell the students that they may play aurally "in sync" with other members of the band if they choose but that it is not required. The only requirement for the students is to be spontaneous and to have fun. If there is extra time, students can trade groups or roles.
- *Note: For the sake of simplicity, the teacher can first prompt the students to perform the activity over a static chord vamp or scale. As the students gain experience with this activity, they can begin to try the concept over a 12-bar blues form with a blues scale or even over a tune's chord changes.*
- There are several educational benefits to this instigation role activity. One such advantage is that there is quite a bit of inherent flexibility to this approach. Instigation roles are not limited to the descriptions just listed. Other possible roles may include "countermelodies," "repeated fast notes," "extremely loud to extremely soft," "funny sounds" (this role can start students on exploring some unusual instrument techniques), or whatever roles the jazz band director can devise. It is easy to perform this activity as a short warm-up that takes five minutes or less.

Assessment

Formative

- Students can write three to four ideas for instigation sounds at home and bring their lists in for rehearsal. Peers trade ideas and provide feedback identifying whether the ideas address register, dynamics, articulation, sequences, and so on.

Summative

- *Note: A summative assessment is not necessary in this exercise because it is an exploratory group exercise.*

Lesson Benefits

- Students can practice improvisation with clear musical "roles."
- Students can practice improvisation with openness and complete freedom in a manner that is less beleaguered than that of a more structured activity
- Students can explore improvisation around a clear musical characteristic (e.g., staccato articulations).
- While basic harmonic understanding is critical to chord-based jazz improvisation, it is possible for students who are constantly drilled on chord changes, scales, arpeggios, and patterns to become a bit "note-centric," which can lead them to ignore the improvisation possibilities inherent in rhythm, dynamics, and articulations. The instigation role activity assigns no chord/scale relationships and invites the students to personally explore their own ways of improvising with rhythms, dynamics, and articulations.

Recordings

- Artist: Jeff Albert's Instigation Quartet
- Recording: *The Tree on the Mound*

Intermediate Jazz Ensemble—*Prayer Meeting From Outer Space (Mingus and Sun Ra)*

Description

Many cultural and technical factors can make young students uncomfortable with improvisation. One major contributing factor is the social pressure of having to do a new activity in the spotlight in front of their peers. Another is the perceived open-ended quality of solo improvisation. Nachmanovitch writes that "if you have all of the colors available, you are sometimes almost too free. With one dimension constrained, play becomes freer in other dimensions" (1991, p. 85). This concept is why many jazz educators have had great success having students improvise on a blues scale or pentatonic scale. By removing many of the complex options, teachers can make the activity seem much less daunting.

Charles Mingus and Sun Ra were two iconic jazz bandleaders and composers who often featured dense, multilayered textures in their ensemble writing. With both composers, these textures often involved a unique combination of composition and improvisation. Butch Morris, an influential figure in group improvisation mentioned later in this section, actually states that Sun Ra was an early influence on his Conduction® (Morris, 2017) ideas.

The purpose of this activity is not to have the student jazz ensemble sound like a Mingus or Sun Ra group but to imitate the multilayered ethos of their recordings. This activity is also meant to engage student differentiation in the jazz ensemble. As most jazz-ensemble teachers know, students differ wildly in their enthusiasm to improvise: some have no problem improvising, while others are simply terrified by the idea. The purpose of this activity is to let each student engage a comfortable individual role (one hopes that after extended experience, he or she will experiment with *other* roles) while contributing to a more adventurous group improvisation.

Materials
Notated chord changes.

Learning Goals
- Students will demonstrate agency and textural improvisation choices by creatively placing repertoire phrases in non-notated sections.
- Students will work with their sections and develop creative placements for phrases from repertoire.
- Section players will develop as leaders in textural improvisation.
- Students will develop greater awareness of how phrases are positioned in terms of melodic texture, rhythm, and range.
- Students will develop their aural, transposition, and metric placement skills.

Procedure
- The first step of this activity is for the teacher to define specific musical "roles" for the ensemble. Examples of these roles can include but are not limited to the following:
  - Soloist
  - Obbligato (usually a florid, ornamental part that plays around the melody or soloist)
  - Riff (a repetitive or riff-based background melody): This can be based on chord tones such as the third, fifth, seventh, and ninth or more melodic/scalar approaches.
  - Possible secondary riff
  - Bass part
  - Drum/rhythmic groove part (if there is auxiliary percussion in the room, students who do not normally play drum set can play the rhythmic groove role with those instruments)
- After the teacher clearly explains the roles to the students, the students should be prompted to organize themselves into groups around these "roles." It is perfectly fine to have instruments from different sections on a single "role" (e.g., Alto 2, Trumpet 4, and Trombone 3 on the obbligato part).
  - These groups should be given the chord changes to a jazz tune (if the teacher wants to "streamline" into concert preparation, she can choose chord changes from

a repertoire tune. A practical first choice for this activity would be a 12-bar blues form at a reasonable tempo).

- Each group should be given time to prepare some musical material that fits their "role" over the chord changes. Those in the "soloist" group should practice soloing over the chord changes and bounce ideas off one another. The "bass part" group can either try to come up with a melodic bassline or simply play the root tones. *Contextual note: this use of roles is actually similar to the approach taken by early New Orleans or Dixieland groups such as Joe Oliver and his Creole Jazz Band and Louis Armstrong's Hot Five and Hot Seven, but Charles Mingus took a looser, more fluid approach to his use of such roles.*

- The groups should be prompted to play their parts separately for the teacher and then to try merging the parts into an integrated whole. The teacher will then prompt the students to figure out a sequence for these parts to lead to a rough arrangement.

- Throughout this process, the teacher should act as the "guide on the side," walking around the room and providing musical suggestions when needed or asked.

- This is the starting place for this activity. The purpose is to let different students engage improvisation at different levels of comfort. Eventually, the teacher should encourage students to try participating in other groups (if a student is very nervous to improvise, this adjustment might be as simple as a move from the "bass part" group to the "riff" group). If a student does not want to switch groups, he should not be forced.

Assessment

Formative

- After one section has improvised according to the given guidelines, the teacher asks students to reflect on what fit or what felt awkward. Students in other sections are also invited to reflect on the combinations of sounds that were in the foreground versus the background. The teacher should feel free to point out interesting combinations that students may not have heard, or to give them performance tips for moving through awkward moments. The reflective process should be repeated for each improvising section.

Summative

- The teacher asks students to listen to one of the tracks from the Charles Mingus or Sun Ra recordings listed later in this section and write an essay, report, or analysis on a track. In particular, a formal analysis/diagram can be a great way for students to understand all of the textural possibilities in group improvisation (obviously the teacher would have to guide the students as to what to include in the formal analysis). The teacher assesses the assignment on the level of detail that students provide in regard to textural changes.

Lesson Benefits

- Students can participate in an improvisation activity without being singled out for solo improvisation.
- Students can demonstrate agency as part of a group textural improvisation without feeling under pressure to generate novel melodies, rhythms, or lines.
- Students can engage musical constructs/abilities other than reading music, including playing by ear, phrase structure awareness, and transposition.

Recordings

Please visit the Oxford University Press Companion Website for Listening Examples 9.1–9.6 ⏵ *of a college jazz ensemble performing this activity. Examples include students in the musical roles of soloist, obbligato, riff, groove, and bass, and the final example features a combined improvisation.*

- Artist: Charles Mingus
- Recording: *Mingus Ah Um*

- Artist: Charles Mingus
- Recording: *Blues & Roots*

- Artist: Mingus Big Band
- Recording: *Mingus Big Band 93: Nostalgia in Times Square*

- Artist: Sun Ra Arkestra (For new Sun Ra listeners, much of his recorded output will sound very chaotic. We recommend starting with these two recordings and then branching out to others if so desired)
- Recording: *Jazz in Silhouette*

- Artist: Sun Ra Arkestra
- Recording: *Languidity*

Beginning Improvisation Ensemble—*Imitation of Found Sounds*

Description

This lesson takes the idea of a found sounds and prompts students to listen to their environments and imitate those sounds that most intrigue them. To inspire them to imagine the possibilities, the teacher should have the students listen to recordings that are based on the manipulation of found sounds and then invite the students to record sounds in their own environment and to imitate and sculpt these sounds during improvisations. This lesson is distinct from the "Nontraditional Sounds" lesson in that students are specifically prompted to *imitate* natural sounds that they hear as part of everyday life.

Materials

- Recorded examples (see the "Recordings" section).
- Students' recordings of found sounds.

Learning Goals

- Students, by using their voice or instruments, will be able to reproduce sounds from their everyday environments.
- Students will be able to describe the timbres found in their environments and use compositional devices to manipulate these sounds.
- Students will imitate and improvise on found sounds in a group improvisation performance.

Procedure

- Begin by having students listen to a found sound composition, such as Marc Ainger's *Shatter.* Though the recording is based on a digital manipulation of several found sounds, the main found sound is shattered glass. Discuss how Ainger musically manipulates these sounds across time, particularly how he features the timbre, extends it, and layers with other sounds to create texture.
- Discuss the movie *Looper,* released in 2012. The story is centered around issues of time travel, and the movie score is based on the manipulation of found sounds. Have students listen to *A Body That Technically Does Not Exist.* The composer recorded the rattle of the cage of an old standard room fan, and this became the prominent found sound of the entire soundtrack. How does he set the sound in this soundtrack? What sounds juxtapose it? Does it change dynamically? Why does this sound work particularly well with the idea of time travel?
- Have students break into groups of four to five and use everyday items in the classroom with varying timbres to create group improvisations. Students should think about some of the techniques used in the recordings to manipulate their found sounds, and decide as a group on one to two ideas that they would like to implement. Groups then implement these concepts in improvisations with the found sounds.
- After all the groups have performed, ask students to bring in recordings of found sounds from their home environment. Students should also use a journal to document where they collected the sound and how a given sound compares to other sounds in its actual environment. The student should then make a second recording that includes an imitation of the sound either by voice or instrument. Both recordings should be brought to the next class.
- In the next class, students share their recordings of found sounds in their small groups and their ideas for imitating those sounds. Students demonstrate the manipulation of their sounds to one another.

- Group members perform a group improvisation in which they imitate the found sounds by using their voices or instruments and choose parameters for layering in at the beginning and out at the end. As the piece progresses each student is responsible for implementing various manipulations of her sound at appropriate times.
- Students comment on one another's group improvisations and try to guess the sounds that the other groups were trying to imitate and manipulate.

Assessment

Formative

- Students improvise in groups on their imitation of found sounds. Each group listens to the other groups and provides feedback on their improvised performances. The teacher and students should identify unique ways that each group manipulated the sounds, and draw connections to the recordings they listened to earlier in class. The teacher or students should also try to provide at least one suggestion for future improvisations.

Summative

- All the students submit recordings of their found sounds, imitation of found sounds, and a journal entry on their experience with those sounds as well as ideas for altering them. The teacher assesses whether students have thoughtfully reflected on the found sound through imitation and writing, and the number of ideas or depth of ideas that they have presented for altering the found sound.

Lesson Benefits

- Students will listen to the sounds of their everyday environments with heightened awareness.
- Students will think beyond the traditional sounds of instruments.
- Improvisations on found sounds can also be part of a bigger unit on computer compositions based on found sounds (see "Studio Magic" in the lesson on "Dynamics").
- Students think individually about sculpting their own sounds.

Recordings

- Artist: Marc Ainger
- Recording: *Shatter*
- Source: https://soundcloud.com/ainger

- Artist: Nathan Johnson
- Recording: *Looper* (original motion picture soundtrack)
- Song: "A Body That Technically Does Not Exist"

Intermediate Improvisation Ensemble—*Gesticulation*

Description

This lesson involves an individual informally conducting a group of individuals through a series of hand gestures. Improvisation comes into play both through the choices of the conductor and the way that the musicians choose to interpret his or her hand gestures. "Gesticulation" is influenced by Conduction® (Morris, 2017), a form of group improvisation pioneered through codified hand and baton gestures compiled by jazz cornetist and composer, Butch Morris.

Materials

- Although, for the sake of simplicity, this activity encourages the "conductor" to use informal, spontaneous hand gestures, we strongly recommend that the reader visit www.conduction.us to observe the brilliant system of gestures compiled by Butch Morris.
- Online videos of Bobby McFerrin's audience interaction workshops
  - Spontaneous Inventions, https://www.youtube.com/watch?v=5VfyMPHzYdQ
  - Notes and Neurons, https://www.youtube.com/watch?v=SZEjUhJ_nPc

Learning Goals

- Students will communicate musical ideas through physical gestures.
- Students will interpret musical ideas through physical gestures.
- Students will move from improvising musical ideas to purposefully sculpting musical sounds into a composition.

Procedure

- Students should sit in a semicircle so that a conductor can face an individual student or a small group of students and communicate conducting gestures. *Note: More specifically, this organization can mean avoiding "layer" rows of students as one often finds in an orchestra.*
- The individual who is doing the "conducting" should be encouraged to use eye contact and intuitive hand gestures to cue the musicians in the ensemble. Since the gestures and cues are not explicit directions in the form of written notes or rhythms, the musicians will interpret the gestures in the form of intuitive sounds. The fun in this activity is that the sounds produced by the musicians often will not match those conceived by the conductor. In this way, it invites the conductor to spontaneously respond to the sounds produced by the musicians. *Note: This type of "conducting" is purely intuitive and does not require formal training in the sense of conducting a symphony orchestra.*

- Sometimes it can be difficult for students to imagine how they could sculpt sounds (not yet known) by using hand gestures. As a result, the teacher may want to model this activity for students.
- Students need to be reminded that they have creative agency in interpreting the conductor's gesture.
- After observing the teacher, individual students will be asked to lead the group in a performance.
- After each performance, the teacher asks the students how the conductor varied or layered sounds. What worked well? The teacher asks the conductor whether he was imagining and trying to achieve certain sound combinations. What worked well for each conductor? And what was surprising or challenging?
- The teacher should video record students as they lead these activities.
- *Note: Unlike many of the "process over product" activities that we have outlined, this can actually be a very fun performance product. Every time that we perform this activity, we ask audience members to come up and conduct the ensemble. Every time we give this prompt to the audience, hands shoot up and we get more volunteers than we can possibly fit in the allotted time. If you teach at a school and your students enjoy this activity, try performing it at a concert. Try inviting parents, other teachers, even the principal up to conduct the group. This effort can yield rewards in terms of community enthusiasm for your music program.*

Advanced version: As students become comfortable with the process, the conductor can become a co-performer and move toward becoming more of a participant/composer. The conductor not only conducts using hand gestures, but she also provides ostinatos, sings descants above the group, or can stomp out a repeating rhythm. The conductor become active in building the piece from her musicianship—conceptualizing the textures and timbres. For inspiration, students can watch videos of Bobby McFerrin in his audience-interaction workshops.

Assessment

Formative

- The teacher asks questions such as the following after each activity iteration: What worked well? What were you imagining and trying to achieve through certain sound combinations? What worked well for the group? And, what was surprising or challenging? *Note: The teacher or performers then provide verbal feedback for refining or clarifying gestures in another version of the experience.*

Summative

- Students review a video of themselves leading a performance and use the self-assessment chart (Figure 3.21) to describe the relationship between their gestures and the

Description of Gesture	Description of Group Response
1.	
2.	
3.	
4.	
5.	
6.	
What part of the performance went as you anticipated?	**What part of the performance surprised you?**

FIGURE 3.21 *Assessment:* Gesticulation self-assessment chart

timbres and textures that were created. The teacher assesses the depth and breadth of the reflection.

Lesson Benefits
- Students have individual opportunity to create timbre and sculpt texture while still improvising.
- Students explore a new musical role.
- Students can take on a more sophisticated role in the advanced version of this exercise by being conductor, composer, and co-performer.

Recordings/Videos
- Website: www.conduction.us

- Artist: Butch Morris
- Recording: *Dust to Dust*

- Online videos of Bobby McFerrin in his interactive audience workshops.
  - Spontaneous Inventions, https://www.youtube.com/watch?v=5VfyMPHzYdQ
  - Notes and Neurons, https://www.youtube.com/watch?v=SZEjUhJ_nPc

Articulation

Beginning Instrumental/Choral Ensemble—
An Articulated Line

Description

This activity invites beginning ensemble members to explore articulation by improvising on melodic and accompaniment lines within familiar repertoire. An important aspect of the experience is for ensemble members to listen and respond to changes other ensemble members make to the statement of a line. The emphasis is on exploration and discussion. The purpose of the activity is to hone students' awareness of the spectrum of articulations and particularly how articulations can change the expression of musical ideas, just as articulations can change the expression of a text. This lesson could also become part of a larger collaborative unit with a language arts or drama teacher on dramatic readings of important literary works.

Materials

- Excerpt from a literary text that appropriately relates to the age group of students.
- Melody or accompaniment sections from any familiar concert repertoire.

Learning Goals

- Students will begin to aurally and physically grasp a fuller conception of the spectrum of articulations.
- Students will begin to grasp some of the natural or typical articulations for particular melodic/rhythmic figures.
- Students will begin to engage in musical play through articulation exploration.
- Students will draw comparisons between articulating lines in music with articulating lines of text.

Procedure

- The teacher begins by reading a famous line from a literary text: for instance, from J. K. Rowling's *Harry Potter and the Sorcerer's Stone*:

  > Mr. and Mrs. Dursley, of number four, Privet Drive, were proud to say that they were perfectly normal, thank you very much. They were the last people you'd expect to be involved in anything strange or mysterious, because they just didn't hold with such nonsense (Rowling, 1997, p. 1).

- The teacher reads the lines again but with varying articulations. For example,

  > [*The teacher starts with smooth articulation.*] Mr. and Mrs. Dursley, of number four, Privet Drive, were proud to say that they were perfectly normal, [*continues on but with short articulation*] thank you very much. [*Continues on but with gliding articulation.*] They were the last people you'd expect to be involved in anything strange or mysterious, [*continues on with march-like articulation*] because they just didn't hold with such nonsense. (Rowling, 1997, p. 1).

- The teacher introduces students to a list of adjectives (e.g., smooth, jumpy, pointed, gliding, marching, skipping, and floating) on the board and asks students to identify what articulations they heard in the reading.
- The teacher then draws the comparison of the articulation of a text to the articulation of a melody from the students' concert repertoire. The teacher performs an excerpt from the concert repertoire. improvising articulations every four bars, and then asks, "What did you enjoy? What surprised you?" The teacher should listen attentively to students' comments.
- Students are then invited to improvise articulations to a section of music from the concert repertoire all together at one time. They can use the adjectives on the board, or create new ideas. This approach may initially sound a little chaotic but it allows students to feel safe during exploration. It is best to choose a section where accompaniment students have a moving harmony so that they have enough time to explore articulations.
- After the group performance, the teacher asks two volunteers to perform the melody and asks one student to perform the accompaniment. Then she asks others to identify what they enjoyed, what surprised them, and how the overall feeling of the line changed. The teacher repeats this process and also prompts students to notice whether duos start improvising articulations off each other.
- Finally, the teacher has the students listen to the suggested recordings to hear how professional artists create different interpretations on the same work by varying their articulations.

Alternative Lesson for Sectionals

- The class follows the first *three* steps listed previously.
- The teacher then breaks students into instrumental or vocal sections to practice an important melody or accompaniment. The teacher asks students to sit in a circle so they can hear one another and make comments at the end of the improvised sections.
- Three to four students play the melody/accompaniment in four-bar chunks in consecutive order. Each student is to play his chunk of the melody with a different articulation, and the melody/harmony should be played straight through without pauses between individuals. The activity works best if the part each student is working on is at least 12 measures, giving a group of three at least four bars to improvise articulations.
- Students can reference adjectives on the board as a starting point for their improvisations, but they should not feel limited to those suggestions.
- After one group has performed, other section members should comment on what they enjoyed or what surprised them in the new performances of the melody/accompaniment. This exercise will work best if the teacher has thoroughly modeled this type of dialogue and listening at the start of the activity.
- After all students have improvised on the melody, the teacher asks groups to select one articulation they heard for each of the improvised chunks. For instance, they may have liked someone playing pointed articulations in measures 1–4, gliding articulations in measures 5–8, and marching articulations in bars 9–12. Students should write in the descriptions for their articulations and practice them as a group. For example, students might agree that a pointy sound is appropriate for one chunk and write that description in their music.
- The teacher brings the sections back together and has them perform their new articulations for the ensemble. If certain groups have melodies/harmonies that happen at the same time in the music, the teacher has the sections play together to hear how the newly articulated lines fit together. The teacher should ask students how their edited versions change the feeling of the piece.
- Finally, the teacher can play any of the recommended recordings to demonstrate how artists often play with articulation to create different interpretations of music.

Assessment

Formative

- The teacher listens during the discussion about the dramatic reading and performance to determine whether students have a sufficient understanding of articulation before asking them to improvise. If necessary, the teacher models more articulations in another performance to broaden their understanding of articulation before their improvisations.

- The students provide feedback to one another on improvised musical ideas that they enjoyed in their melodies or accompaniments, and make decisions about possible interpretations that they all could take in their small groups.

Summative

- After student groups have played their newly articulated sections together, the teacher has students write a reflection comparing the way the music was originally articulated with their new interpretation. What was gained? What was lost, if anything? The teacher assesses students on the depth of their comparisons.
- Students can complete a Frayer Model slip (Figure 3.22), a common assessment used by literacy specialists, on a given adjective or term. Students can be prompted to include musical examples from the repertoire, along with verbal descriptions.

Lesson Benefits

- Students can creatively explore the entire spectrum of musical articulations.
- Students can playfully apply divergent creativity to their regular ensemble repertoire.
- Students draw comparison between the articulation of text and the articulation of music.
- Students can learn literary terms and descriptors within the experiential context of music.

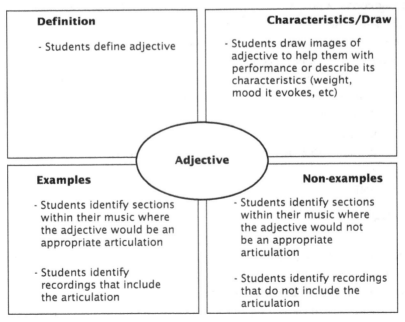

FIGURE 3.22 *Assessment:* Frayer Model for adjectives

Recordings

Any recordings that feature two interpretations of the same piece.

- Artist: Glenn Gould
- Piece: J. S. Bach's *Goldberg Variations*
- Recordings: 1955 and 1981 recordings

- Composer: J. S. Bach
- Piece: *Six Solo Suites for Cello*
- Sample performers: Erling Blöndal Bengtsson and Pablo Casals

- Artist: Joni Mitchell
- Song: "Both Sides Now"
- Recordings: *Clouds* (1969) and *Both Sides Now* (2000)

- Composer: Gnarls Barkley
- Song: "Crazy"
- Recordings: Gnarls Barkley's original version on *St. Elsewhere* and Ray LaMontagne's cover on https://www.youtube.com/watch?v=6mEfDSP4g_U

- Song: "Bye Bye Blackbird" (by Ray Henderson)
- Recordings: Ben Webster/Oscar Peterson, *Ben Webster Meets Oscar Peterson*; Miles Davis, *Round About Midnight*; Clark Terry/Bob Brookmeyer Quintet, *Gingerbread Men*

Intermediate Instrumental/Choral Ensemble—*Pointillism*

Description

The purpose of this activity is for individual players to use articulations to imitate the visual art form commonly known as "pointillism" (e.g., the artwork of Georges Seurat) as part of a group improvisation.

Materials

Visuals of pointillist paintings. *Note: See the following list as a starting point.*

- Georges Seurat, *The Circus*
- Georges Seurat, *A Sunday Afternoon on the Island of La Grande Jatte*
- Paul Signac, *The Grand Canal (Venice)*
- Paul Signac, *The Papal Palace, Avignon*
- Vincent Van Gogh, *Self-Portrait* [1887]
- Georges Lemmen, *Beach at Heist*
- Georges Lemmen, *Clear Night, Moon*

Note: Imitation of pointillism invariably leads to a focus on short articulations (staccato, marcato). The advanced version of this activity involves a transition from articulations that imitate pointillism to articulations that imitate the broad stroke differences of abstract expressionism (e.g., Jackson Pollock). The following is a list of abstract expressionist masterpieces that serve as a starting point for teachers.

- Jackson Pollock, *White Light* [A particular favorite of saxophonist and improviser Ornette Coleman]
- Jackson Pollock, *Untitled (Green Silver)* [Another favorite of Ornette Coleman]
- Helen Frankenthaler, *Mountains and Sea*
- Norman Lewis, *Jazz Band*
- Elaine de Kooning, *Bullfight*
- John Marin, *Region of Brooklyn Bridge Fantasy*
- Wassily Kandinsky, *Moscow I. Red Square*

Learning Goals
- The students will experiment with a variety of articulations.
- The students will aurally identify and imitate articulations in a larger ensemble texture.
- The students will create various ensemble textures by employing different articulations.

Procedure
- The basic premise of the activity is that individual students should perform distinct articulations that produce a collective texture in the ensemble. This should be similar to a pointillist painting wherein the individual's minute brush strokes create a larger image.
- To acclimate students to this process in a gradual way, the teacher can prompt the students to perform staccato or marcato articulations on a different predetermined rhythm for each musician or section. See Figure 3.23 for clarification.
- If the teacher and/or student prefers pitch guidelines, the teacher can present a common scale or pitch set for every student to use. The possibilities are virtually endless but could include examples such as the following:
  1. Major
  2. Relative minor
  3. Melodic minor (ascending or descending)
  4. Harmonic minor
  5. Modal scales (Dorian, Phrygian, Lydian, etc.)
  6. Diminished/octatonic
  7. Whole tone
  8. Pentatonic
  9. Random pitch sets such as F, B♭, C♯, E. *Note: This guideline can be turned into an activity in which students raise their hands and volunteer pitch names.*

INSTRUCTIONS: Teacher assigns a scale or pitch set. Each student selects one of the eight rhythms and can use any notes from the scale or pitch set as long as they perform the selected rhythm. Examples #5 and #7 include tenuto markings to contrast the staccato articulations. *Student repeats the rhythm according to the guidelines of either Conduction or Deep Listening.*

FIGURE 3.23 "Pointillism" rhythm chart

- There are two different ways a teacher can direct this activity:
  1. *Gesticulation:* The same rules established in the aforementioned "Gesticulation" activity in the "Texture and Timbre" section of this book still apply except the teacher or student conductor is encouraged to use hand gestures that imply short, staccato, or jagged articulations.
  2. *Deep listening:* (See the "Deep Listening" activity in the Dynamics section of this book.) The same rules established in the deep-listening activity still apply except the students should "catch" and "pass" staccato sounds.

Assessment

Formative
If the teacher approaches this activity like "Gesticulation," then the following applies:

- The teacher asks questions like the following after each conductor and group: What worked well? What were you imagining and trying to achieve through certain articulation combinations? How did the group respond to you as a conductor? What worked well for the group? And what was surprising or challenging? The teacher or performers then provide verbal feedback for refining or clarifying gestures in another experience.
- If the teacher approaches this activity like the "Deep Listening" exercise, the same questions from the previous point can be used. But the teacher should also ask this question: How did you as a group respond to one another?

Summative
- The teacher prompts students to write a short paper on a pointillist/abstract expressionist artist and compare a recent group improvisation to that artist's work. The teacher assesses students' ability to transfer ideas on stroke and style to articulations discussed and performed in class.
- The teacher requests small groups to record themselves aurally imitating a particular painting through this activity. Other groups listen to the recording and look at the painting to determine connections between the works. Students write a reflection on the articulation connections and the teacher assesses the students' ability to transfer ideas on stroke and style to articulations in the recorded group performance.

Lesson Benefits
- The students can creatively explore the nuances of the articulation spectrum.
- The students can creatively use articulations to participate in improvising collective textures without being asked to solo in isolation.

Recordings
- Artist: The Jazz Mandolin Project
- Recording: *Jungle Tango*
- Song: "Pointillism"

- Composer: Igor Stravinsky
- Piece: *The Rite of Spring*
- Movement: "Augurs of Spring"

- Artist: Joe Lovano/Gunther Schuller
- Recording: *Rush Hour*

Beginning Jazz Ensemble—*Cartoon Sounds*

Description

Many older cartoons referenced big band music for both their soundtracks and sound effects. While they may not be exactly identical, many jazz articulations utilize embellishments that are similar to those of cartoon sound effects. Examples include marcato quarter notes (distinct from staccato notes), pitch bends, elaborate glissandi, and embellished slurs. The purpose of this activity is to use cartoon sound effects as inspiration for articulation and timbral improvisation. The students should be encouraged to have fun and use articulations and sound effects that match the action in the cartoon.

Materials

Videos of any age-appropriate cartoons.

Learning Goals

- The students will explore and experiment with different articulations on their instruments.
- The students will explore and experiment with different timbres on their instruments.

Procedure

- The teacher should begin by describing and demonstrating a few of the ways that students can imitate cartoon sounds through embellished articulations and expressions. Examples can include a trombone glissando, playing trills on a saxophone, and playing on the bell of a crash cymbal. The teacher should not delegate too much; the purpose of this activity is exploration and experimentation.
- The teacher should play a muted clip of an age-appropriate cartoon for the students. Older cartoons with lots of slapstick (e.g., Looney Tunes, Disney) tend to work better for this activity. The teacher should let the students watch the clip without playing so they can observe the events.
- The teacher should play the clip again and ask the students to experiment with sounds on their instruments that seem to fit the cartoon slapstick.
- The teacher should play the clip again for the students with the sound on so that they can hear what sounds and music are actually used for the clip.
- The teacher should play the clip one more time with muted sound so that the students can draw inspiration from their personal experimentation *and* the sounds they heard in the actual clip.

Assessment

Formative

- The teacher begins a conversation on students' performance for the clip with the following questions: What worked well? What did not fit? What could be done differently?

Group suggestions are then used to refine students' performance with the clip. If a student had a sound in mind but was having trouble executing it, the teacher can provide some guidance.

Summative

- The teacher asks students to write a reflection or report on one of the recommended recordings. The teacher assesses the reflection on the basis of the sound effects that the student noticed.
- If students happen to have advanced computer/digital recording skills for their age, they can record their music/sound effects for a clip and then use a program such as iMovie or YouTube to insert the sound file into the clip. If the teacher has expertise in this area, he or she can assist students who may want to do so. The teacher would assess the alignment of sounds with the cartoon as well as how the sounds affect the overall story plot.

Lesson Benefits

- Students partake in fun musical *play*.
- Students can explore unique timbres, articulations, and sound effects that they may not have explored in the context of their ensemble's repertoire.

Recordings

- Artist: Raymond Scott
- Recording: *The Music of Raymond Scott: Reckless Nights and Turkish Twilights*

- Artist: Don Byron
- Recording: *Bug Music*

- Artist: Carl Stalling
- Recording: *The Carl Stalling Project*

- Artist: John Zorn
- Recording: *Cartoon/S&M*

- Artist: Sun Ra
- Recording: *Space Is the Place*

The following is the aforementioned list of performers who excelled at nontraditional sound effects:
- Voice: Bobby McFerrin, The Element Choir
- Violin: Mark O'Connor, Zach Brock
- Cello: Matt Turner
- Bass: Avishai Cohen (upright), Victor Wooten (electric)
- Flute: Rahsaan Roland Kirk, Jamie Baum
- Clarinet: Don Byron

- Saxophone: James Carter, Pharoah Sanders, Joseph Jarman
- Trumpet: Clark Terry, Cootie Williams, Lester Bowie, Steven Bernstein
- Trombone: Ed Neumeister, Roswell Rudd, Jeffrey Albert
- Piano: Cecil Taylor, Myra Melford
- Guitar: Derek Bailey, Bill Frisell, Pat Metheny
- Drums: Matt Wilson, Ed Blackwell, Tyshawn Sorey
- Mallet percussion: Gary Burton, Kevin Norton, Peyton MacDonald

Intermediate Jazz Ensemble—*Articulate the Positive*

Description

One of the most difficult concepts many students encounter when trying to improvise "straight-ahead jazz" is mastering the articulations perfected by jazz greats. Rhythm and articulation should be a combined focus for this activity, which uses Figure 3.12, "Jazz Rhythm Syllabus," from the "Blues" section of "Harmony." One of the reasons that straight-ahead jazz language eludes many young students is that the combination of the chord/scale relationships, swing feel, rhythmic placement, articulation, instrumental technique, listening, and creativity form an extremely complex, sometimes overwhelming construct. The purpose of this exercise is for students to explore the spectrum of embellishment in jazz articulations by experimenting with them in a low-pressure, group texture.

Materials

- "Jazz Rhythm Syllabus," Figure 3.12.
- Jazz ensemble repertoire

Learning Goals

- Students will begin to actively explore the spectrum of jazz articulation embellishments for common jazz rhythms.

Procedure

- This activity can be approached with a strategy that is similar to "Techno Music" (as found in this "Articulation" section).
- The teacher should begin by reviewing some of the articulations and rhythms from Figure 3.12, "Jazz Rhythm Syllabus." If the students prefer to use rhythms from their jazz ensemble repertoire, that approach works just as well.
- For the first few iterations of this activity, the teacher should line up a few students in order. The teacher should set a tempo, a style (i.e., swing, Latin, funk) and give the students a *repeating* chord, scale, or simple progression as the basis for the activity (e.g., C Dorian, G major, ii^7–V^7–I, or a 12-bar blues form). *Note: Rhythm section participants*

can either provide the accompaniment or participate in the activity in the same manner as the other wind instruments. After the teacher has determined the chord, scale, or progression as well as the number of measures, each student in line should try to come up with a clearly articulated rhythm that repeats in the exact same section every time (it does not matter whether this is every measure, every two measures, or every four measures). *Note: The key to this activity is that each student should experiment with some of the articulations from the "Jazz Rhythm Syllabus" with different degrees of embellishment.*

- The next student in line should add another rhythm that adds another layer to the mix. By the time that all of the students have added their respective rhythms, there should be a reasonably full group texture. *The students are allowed to alter their rhythm, but we would not recommend that a student change it dramatically before every student has had the opportunity to enter. Remember that students are entering the fray with specific textures in mind; it might throw them off if other students change the rhythmic content on them.*

- The teacher should encourage the students to experiment with some eighth-note ideas, since a mix of effective eighth-note rhythms and articulations is the recipe for a nuanced swing feel.

- The teacher's musical feedback is critical to students' learning success in this activity. Instead of telling a student that he did it "wrong" or she should play a different rhythm/articulation, the teacher should try to provide constructive feedback as to how the student can shape the rhythm/articulation with more nuance. Some sample responses along these lines might include the following:
  - "Very good. Try putting more accent on that marcato note."
  - "Terrific. Try putting less space between your eighth notes."
  - "Excellent. Try slurring every other eighth-note pair starting on the upbeat."

- If the student is still confused, the teacher can either model the rhythm/articulation or play a recording with a nuanced example.

Assessment

Formative

- In this activity, it is important that the teacher give prompt and constructive feedback. See the suggestions for phrasing feedback in the "Procedures" section. After a student has applied the suggestions, the teacher should ideally provide feedback and/or ask the student what felt different.

Summative

- The teacher can assign a very short transcription activity (e.g., four measures of a Louis Armstrong solo) in which the students are responsible for writing down the jazz artist's notes, rhythms, and articulations. The teacher assesses the students' ability to identify and notate articulations.

Lesson Benefits

- Students can explore the integration of jazz articulations and rhythms in a low-pressure group environment.
- Students can experiment with the spectrum of jazz articulation embellishment.
- Students practice jazz articulation without concerning themselves with intense concentration on chord changes, chord/scale relationships, or tune form.

Recordings

- For examples of nuanced jazz articulations, the teacher and students should go to the source by listening to the recordings of jazz greats. This is just a small list of these figures that only scratches the surface:
  - *"Straight Ahead" Jazz:* Louis Armstrong, Lester Young, Jack Teagarden, Buddy Rich, Ray Brown, Harry "Sweets" Edison, Wes Montgomery, Red Garland, Charlie Parker, Art Blakey, Paul Chambers, Sonny Rollins, Jim Hall, Oscar Peterson, Miles Davis, J. J. Johnson, Chet Baker
  - *Latin Jazz*: Arturo Sandoval, Paquito D'Rivera, Conrad Herwig, Poncho Sanchez, Bobby Sanabria, Danilo Perez, Chucho Valdes
  - *Rock/funk/fusion:* Weather Report [group], Pat Metheny, The Yellowjackets [group], Tower of Power [group], The Brecker Brothers [group], David Sanborn, Miles Davis (after 1970)
- Examples of this sort of textural improvisation:
  - Artist: Bill Holman Band
  - Recording: *A View From the Side*

  - Artist: Machito
  - Recording: *Machito at the Crescendo*

  - Artist: Tower of Power
  - Recording: *The Very Best of Tower of Power*

Beginning Improvisation Ensemble— *Articulated Movement*

Description

When you look at the great dancers of the world, an incredible amount of information is captured in the articulations of their bodies. The arch and landing of Martha Graham's feet in her solo *Lamentations,* or the salutation in Farruquito's flamenco dancing integrate concepts of flow, weight, energy, and use of space. Through movement, students can begin to understand that articulation is not just about the sound of staccato or legato but about the approach to achieve these sounds. This activity takes inspiration from creative dance and uses movement as a prompt for musical improvisations. As students musically improvise to movements, they explore articulation as integrally connected to dynamics, tempo, and register.

Materials
Space for movement.

Learning Goals
- Students will make connections between movement elements and musical elements.
- Students will create movement pieces that demonstrate flow, weight, energy, and use of space.
- Students will improvise music to the movement pieces and explore articulation, dynamics, tempo, and register.
- Students will identify music that aligns well with movements, and will make suggestions for improvement.

Procedure
- The teacher asks students to create small groups of five to seven students.
- Each group will (1) create a movement piece, and (2) observe another movement group and improvise accompanying music.
- Students should use their bodies to demonstrate different aspects of flow (smooth, jagged), weight (heavy, light), energy (fast, slow), and space (high, medium, low). We recommend that the piece last a minimum of 30 seconds to a maximum of one minute.
- Students will very likely need some guidance to begin. For example, each student could choose a movement that is his own, and his movement must seamlessly transition into the next person's movement. The opposite would be that the group work together the entire time to demonstrate different concepts throughout the group performance. Or students can intermix their composition to include solo movement with group movement. *Note: If students are very inhibited about movement, they can also musically improvise to some of the listed video resources.*
- Once students have a sense of their movements, they should decide on different lengths of time for the movements. Movements do not need to happen for proportionate amounts of time. In fact, it makes it more interesting if the movements are not choreographed like eight beat phrases in many dances. To feel some consistency, students can be encouraged to feel an underlying pulse that unifies transitions between movements.
- Once groups have practiced their movement compositions, they then perform their pieces for another student group. The observing student group ideally has a number of classroom instruments available to them, including pitched and non-pitched percussion instruments, as well as keyboards. But if these instruments are not available, students can use their voices and found sounds in the classroom.
- We recommend that the student movement groups perform twice before the observing group is invited to improvise to the movements. The observing group

should not discuss what they are going to musically play beforehand. The first accompaniment should be purely improvisational. After the improvisation, the instrumentalists should identify how the music articulated the movements, and whether there was anything missing. The movement group can also be encouraged to discuss what music they noticed in response to their movements. After the initial performance, students can try the improvisation, once again trying to refine their performance.

- After the first group has gone, the preceding process should be repeated with student groups performing their movement pieces for other improvising observation groups.

- *Extension:* Students can be challenged to create a larger improvised composition. For instance, if there are three student groups, the composition takes on an A, B, C structure, with connecting bridge music that facilitates transitions for students to move between their creative movement roles and improvisations. Students should be challenged to keep a musical thread going that starts when they observe the movements of group A. This improvised musical thread connects the sections and creates a compositional whole. We have found that the musical thread is best when students find it in the moment of performance.

Assessment

Formative

- Students demonstrate their understanding of flow, weight, energy and use of space as they work in small groups. The teacher can challenge students to think about a particular concept if they are not depicting it throughout their movement compositions.

- Students demonstrate their understanding of flow, weight, energy, and use of space by translating those ideas into improvisations that include but are not limited to articulation, dynamics, tempo, and register.

Summative

- Students watch videos of their movement pieces with improvised music. Using the "Articulated Movement Table" (Figure 3.24), they describe the connections between the movement concepts and the musical concepts to translate the ideas of flow, weight, energy, and use of space to articulation, dynamics, tempo, and register. At the end of the document, there is also space for observations they can make about the relationships between concepts. For instance, a student may notice that upper-register notes were always played with a light striking sound, or that continuous rapid movements sounded smooth. If so desired, these observations invite future dialogue on performance practice and limitations on instruments in regard to articulations.

Video Time	Movement Concepts: Flow, weight, energy, space	Musical Concepts: Articulation, dynamics, tempo, register
Did you notice any connections between the movement or musical concepts?		

FIGURE 3.24 Articulated Movement Table

Movement Pieces to Watch

- Martha Graham, *Lamentations*
  https://www.youtube.com/watch?v=Pb4-kpClZns

- Antonio Canales, "Casa Patas, flamenco en vivo #303"
  https://www.youtube.com/watch?v=IhwwWfhAYWQ

- Farruquito, "Improvisation" (flamenco)
  https://www.youtube.com/watch?v=rNc7aXApUdA

- Hubbard Street Dance Company, "Cloudless" by Alejandro Cerrudo
  https://www.youtube.com/watch?v=iEgcff5020Q

- Alvin Ailey Dance Company, "Revelations" by Alvin Ailey
  https://www.youtube.com/watch?v=tNqaixKbrjs

Recordings (Highlighting Articulations)

- Composer: Sufjan Stevens
- Recording: *Age of Adz*
- Piece: "Vesuvius"
  Note: The example includes many layers of electronic instruments with varying articulations.

- Composers: Rodgers and Hammerstein
- Piece: "People Will Say We're in Love" from *Oklahoma!*
  Note: The example demonstrates the relationship between smooth articulations and the gliding feeling in waltzes.

- Composer: Mikhail Glinka
- Piece: Overture to *Russlan and Ludmilla*
  Note: The example demonstrates the relationship between tempo and articulation.

Intermediate Improvisation Ensemble—*Techno Music*

Description

Techno house or dance music is distinct for its use of electronically simulated note repetition in the form of grooves. Since techno music makes use of note repetition, there is often a distinct emphasis on digitally performed articulations. For this activity, the students should be encouraged to improvise layers of repeated notes with particular articulations to imitate the sound of techno music. Recorded examples are key for this activity. The teacher should play appropriate examples of artists such as the Propellerheads or the Gorillaz.

Note: This lesson is meant to facilitate a type of responsive group improvisation that embraces articulation experimentation and learning. It is an understatement to say that it barely scratches the surface of the experience produced by nuanced composers, producers, and disk jockeys (DJs). If the students begin to demonstrate particular facility in this activity, the teacher should feel free to encourage them to explore parallel harmony, a key component of much techno music.

Materials
Sample techno basslines

Learning Goals
- Students will explore different types of articulations in a creative improvisatory setting.
- By using brief, repeating rhythms, students will explore how their articulations make up a larger group texture.
- Students will compound on the articulation learning by incorporating difficult rhythms from rehearsal and concert repertoire into the activity.

Procedure
- The teacher should begin by playing exemplary recordings of techno/house music for the students. *Note: The teacher may have students in class who work as DJs or possess extensive knowledge of techno/house music. The teacher can remind these students that*

the key purpose of this activity is for responsive improvisation and that this activity only scratches the surface of techno music. These students can be encouraged to individually pursue a more advanced version of this activity and do some peer teaching with other students.

- Depending on the comfort level, either the teacher or one of the students can play the repeating bassline of one of the techno/house examples. This task can become tiring in a hurry so one might either record a repeating vamp of the bassline or set this line up on a program such as Garageband.

- The teacher should also present an accompanying modal scale. On the basis of a given student's comfort level, each participant can either (a) perform the entire rhythm on a single note, (b) perform the rhythm with a stepwise contour by using the scale, or (c) perform the rhythm with any notes from the scale.

- For the first few iterations of this activity, the teacher should line the students up in order. In general, we recommend a maximum of approximately six students in the line. As the bassline repeats, each student in line should try to come up with a clearly articulated rhythm that repeats at the exact same place every time (it does not matter whether this is every measure, every two measures, or every four measures).

  o The next student in line should add another rhythm that adds another layer to the mix. By the time that all of the students have added their respective rhythms, there should be a reasonably full group texture. *Note: The students are allowed to alter their rhythm, but we would not recommend that a student change it dramatically before every student has had the opportunity to enter. Remember that students are entering the mix with specific textures in mind; it might throw them off if other students change the rhythmic content on them.*

  o After the class has performed this activity a few times, the students can begin to enter the mix at their own discretion instead of in a specified order.

Assessment

Formative

- Students can write brief reflections on a class's improvisation on this activity with suggestions for improvement. The teacher reviews reflections collectively, and returns to the group with suggestions from the students' writings, as well as adaptations to the activity that are based on their understandings and performance.

Summative

- Students can write a paper on recorded examples of techno/house music (e.g., the Gorillaz) and end the paper by suggesting ways that this group/individual's body of work might be incorporated into a class improvisation activity. The teacher assesses the students' ability to identify articulation techniques in techno music and transfer those ideas to improving in-class improvised performances.

- *Advanced extension*: Students can use Garageband or a similar program and create their own techno recording that involves improvised lines/threads or use a movie production program to create a music video. *Note: If some or all of the lines are improvised, there will clearly be some trial and error (i.e., extensive use of the "Delete Loop" function) involved. This error element is fine and should just be worked into the time management planning for the project.* The teacher assesses student work on the basis of their ability to transfer ideas that were discussed and performed in class to their own compositions, and considers the students' ability to layer in a way that is reminiscent of techno music. This experience can be enhanced if peers can provide formative feedback to one another before the summative assessment.

Lesson Benefits
- Students can aurally experiment with different articulations.
- Students can participate in a group improvisation without feeling isolated by extensive solo improvisation.
- Students can creatively participate in a music style that is currently very relevant in popular culture.

Recording
Please visit the Oxford University Press Companion Website Listening Example 10.1 ⏵ *for a staccato articulation example created on Chrome Music Lab "Song Maker."*

- Artist: Avicii
- Album: *True*

- Artist: Amon Tobin (Cujo)
- Album: *Adventures in Foam*

- Artists: Daft Punk
- Album: *Discovery*

- Artists: The Chemical Brothers
- Album: *Exit Planet Dust*

- Artists: Propellerheads
- Album: *Decksanddrumsandrockandroll*

Dynamics

Beginning Instrumental/Choral Ensemble—*"Re"Arranging*

Description

A basic component to all music is the significance of dynamics. Beginners often think in terms of loud and soft and become more nuanced with their understanding of dynamic levels as they progress with their listening and technical abilities. This activity is rooted in compositional decisions and moves to improvisatory responses.

Materials

- Any ensemble music can be used for this activity.
- Recording device.

Learning Goals

- Students will explore dynamics through selectively altering existing dynamics within their parts.
- Students will be able to identify, label, and perform dynamics appropriately.
- Students will learn to listen within their section and across the ensemble to changes in dynamics.
- Students will make artistic decisions about the quality of their student-selected dynamics through discussion and assessment of sectional and whole group performances.

Procedure

Each instrumental/vocal section brainstorms dynamic markings for their section on concert repertoire and writes them in their parts (in pencil). Sections may adopt some of the dynamics given by the composer, but they should also create new dynamic choices that alter the feeling of the piece.

- Instrumental/vocal sections practice the new dynamics created by section members.
- The entire ensemble performs the piece with the revised dynamics, and students are asked to listen to the interplay of dynamics across the ensemble.
- The teacher leads a reflective discussion by using the assessment questions.
- If there is a second performance, the goal will shift and students will need to listen and adopt dynamic levels from across the ensemble. The group will begin by playing their revised dynamic part, but midway through the teacher will point to one group to imitate the dynamics of another group. Students could also be invited to the podium to point to sections and make suggestions for dynamic shifts.
- The teacher leads a reflective discussion by using the assessment questions.

Assessment

Formative
- The teacher can begin discussion with the following prompts:
  ○ What led you to choose dynamics for your part?
  ○ How did your dynamic alterations relate to the dynamic changes in your neighboring section?
  ○ How did changes in the dynamics affect the overall feeling of the piece?
  ○ How did the second performance with responsive dynamics feel different from the first performance?
- The teacher should have students blog or journal their responses.

Summative
- Students perform an altered score. The teacher prompts each student to write a reflection on a recording of the performance. Students self-evaluate their section's performance of written dynamics and describe the outcome of their improvised performance. Journal or blog entries are graded for the level of detailed reflection.

Lesson Benefits
- Students fine-tune their listening across sections and within the ensemble.
- Students have a heightened awareness of how ensemble parts fit together.
- Students can demonstrate and discuss their understandings of dynamics with others.

Recordings
- Artist: Gerald Cleaver
- Recording: *Gerald Cleaver's Detroit*
- Song: "6350"

- Composer: Charles Ives
- Piece: *The Unanswered Question*

- Composer: Carl Orff
- Piece: "O Fortuna" from *Carmina Burana*

- Composer: Antonio Vivaldi
- Piece: "Summer," Allegro non molto from *The Four Seasons*

Intermediate Instrumental/Choral Ensemble— *Deep Listening Dynamics:* An Homage to Pauline Oliveros

Description

Pauline Oliveros's (2005) *Deep Listening* exercises challenge and expand the way we as human beings can perceive and respond to sound. In her book, she contrasts listening as a voluntary yet intentional act, with hearing as a physiological response to sounds in our environment. This activity is influenced by Oliveros's *Deep Listening* exercises but with a focus on dynamics. During the activity, students choose dynamic levels for performance and intentionally listen to and send dynamic levels to others across the ensemble.

Materials

None.

Learning Goals

- Students will be able to play dynamics with proper support.
- Students will be able to hear dynamics across the ensemble and intentionally change dynamic levels.
- Students will be able to monitor and describe changes in dynamics across the ensemble.
- Students will be able to differentiate between listening to dynamics as an audience member and actively engaging in the transformation of dynamics in an ensemble.

Procedure

- The teacher should begin by choosing half the students in each section to participate in the first round of this activity. Choosing half the group allows students to have space to hear across the ensemble. Students who are not participating should listen and monitor changes within the ensemble.
- Each student should begin by picking a note and playing it at any volume. When playing sustained notes, students should take breaths or change bows as needed.
- *Note: The next step is key to this activity.* Students should attempt sensitive listening to a more "distant" section of the ensemble.
- When a student hears a particular note/dynamic combination, she should attempt to reproduce it as identically as possible and "send" it to another section of the ensemble for the process to be repeated.

- Students not performing should monitor the sending and receiving of dynamics across the ensemble.
- At the end, the teacher should have students who were performing and listening discuss what they felt and how they responded to students across the ensemble, while students who were monitors discuss what they heard and noticed.
- The teacher should have the groups then share their observations with one another, to determine if what was felt in performance was the same as what was heard by others.
- The teacher should repeat the exercise with the second group of students.

Assessment

Formative

- The teacher prompts students to discuss how they changed and monitored dynamic levels while performing.
- The teacher prompts students to discuss how they heard dynamic changes across the ensemble as audience members.

Summative

- Students listen to a recording of the performance and, through a blog or journals, compare it to their experiences as audience members of the improvised performance. The teacher should prompt students to consider what is gained and what is lost in being an audience member of a live performance or an audience member of the recording. The teacher grades the students' descriptions on the level of detail in their comparisons.

Lesson Benefits

- Students learn to improvise collectively with dynamics and enhance their aural skills.

Recordings

- Artists: Oliveros, Dempster, Panaioitis
- Piece: *Suiren*
- Recording: Deep Listening

- Artists: Oliveros, Dempster, Panaioitis
- Piece: *Lear*
- Recording: Deep Listening

- Artists: Deep Listening Band
- Piece: Section II: *Lapis Lazuli (Live)*
- Recording: Dunrobin Sonic Gems

Beginning Jazz Ensemble—*Conceptual Scores*

Description

This activity is influenced by the work of the great jazz pianist and educator, David Berkman (2007). It is based on the idea that understanding a range of dynamics requires exploration, discussion of technique, and careful listening. Dynamic achievement also differs between what an individual can perform versus what an ensemble can perform. This activity aims to highlight those differences and help individuals and the ensemble achieve varying dynamic levels with purpose and spontaneity.

Materials

None.

Learning Goals

- Students will be able play dynamics with proper support.
- Students will be able to alter dynamics together by listening across the ensemble.
- Students will be able to evaluate and suggest ways of achieving both subtle and extreme dynamics for an entire ensemble.

Procedure

- Students pick a single pitch that they cannot change. Students have the option of starting or stopping the note as the ensemble performs together.
- As students play their single note, they employ a range of dynamics.
- The teacher gestures a starting and stopping point for the entire ensemble and allows students to play until there are waves of dynamic change.
- After performing continuous notes, the teacher asks students to describe how they achieved the range of dynamics, including such issues as breath support, speed of air, and embouchure control.
- Students repeat the same exercise, but the goal is to be the softest instrument in the ensemble.
- Students repeat the same exercise and steadily try to build the volume to *fff*.
- A very interesting variation on this exercise is to have the students try to play an *ensemble forte* or an *ensemble piano*. The trick of this exercise is achieving the whole through the sum of the parts. More specifically, playing an ensemble forte might mean eight students playing *f*, four students playing *mf*, and two students playing *p*. Either way, it involves a tremendous amount of listening.
- The teacher should discuss with students what they individually did to achieve an ensemble dynamic level, and individual students can take turns coming out of the ensemble to hear how group dynamics are achieved.

Assessment

Formative

- The teacher prompts students to describe how they achieved dynamic changes through informal discussion or in a reflective journal.
- The teacher prompts students to draw an image representing their individual dynamic changes.

- The teacher invites student volunteers to stand up, walk around the ensemble, and identify dynamic changes across the ensemble.

Summative
- Each student submits a one-minute video recording of his performance of one note with the use of a variety of dynamic changes. Students' performances are graded on the instrumental or vocal facility used to execute dynamic changes.

Lesson Benefits
- Young students become more cognizant of and creative with dynamics and also learn to partake in deep listening as part of the larger ensemble.

Recordings
- Artist: Joel Frahm
- Recording: *Sorry, No Decaf*
- Song: "Soul Eyes"

- Composer: George Gershwin
- Piece: *Rhapsody in Blue*

- Composer: Maurice Ravel
- Piece: *Boléro*

- Artist: The Vanguard Jazz Orchestra
- Recording: *Monday Night Live at the Village Vanguard*
- Track: "Willow Tree"

Intermediate Jazz Ensemble—*Swells*

Description
Big band charts often have idiomatic yet challenging dynamics. In one instance, students are to play *forte piano*, and in the next, they have to play a controlled crescendo. In this activity, the teacher uses a series of dynamic phrases within the ensemble's repertoire that students perform in leader-led groups.

Materials
Jazz ensemble's concert repertoire.

Learning Goals
- Students will explore the sonic spectrum of dynamics.
- Students will explore the pace of various dynamic changes.
- Students will listen for dynamics and blend across the ensemble.

Procedure

- The teacher selects groups that perform the same phrase(s) in an arrangement (e.g., Alto Sax 1, Alto Sax 2, Tenor Sax 1, Tenor Sax 2, and Trumpet 2 all play this one phrase so that they will be a single group).
- Each group is assigned a separate single phrase that they play together within a given arrangement in the repertoire. For instance, one group's phrase choice might capture *sforzando* on one note and move to *piano*. Another group's choice may feature *piano* to *fortissimo*; a third group, a decrescendo followed by *forte*; and a fourth group may feature a phrase that includes a decrescendo to *subito piano*.
- Each group should assign a leader (the leader role can rotate).
- The teacher selects a tempo for the arrangement and counts off all of the groups. Each group leader performs her phrase alone and decides when to enter, and how long to pause before re-entering. The group leaders repeat for multiple iterations, experimenting with textured layering of dynamics.
- The group leaders are essentially making their own layered dynamic arrangements, and their group members are listening to when their leader has locked into a dynamic version that creates swells with the other group leaders.
- When group members hear their leader lock into a repeated phrase they jump in and perform the dynamic in the same manner to create large ensemble swells.

Assessment

Formative

- The teacher prompts students to write a description on how their group improvisation evolved by using one dynamic phrase.

Summative

- Students listen to a recording of their ensemble improvisation, and each student writes a reflection on when and where the dynamics reflect the characteristics of the big band piece, and when the dynamics shift into a new amalgamation that reflect the lively interaction of dynamic levels. The teacher grades reflections for the level of detail in their descriptions and how the detail corresponds to the given recording.

Lesson Benefits

- Students experience leadership and listening roles while improvising within the safety of a group.
- Students have opportunities to reflect on their roles through self- or group-assessment.
- Students experience a variety of dynamics improvisation.
- Students have flexibility to improvise across the entire ensemble and within their groups.

Recordings

- Artist: Miles Davis/Gil Evans
- Recording: *Porgy and Bess*
- Song: "Prayer"

- Artist: Maria Schneider Jazz Orchestra
- Recording: *Coming About*
- Song: "Coming About"

- Artist: Buddy Rich Big Band
- Recording: *Big Swing Face*
- Song: "Big Swing Face"

- Artist: Louie Bellson and Explosion
- Recording: *Note Smoking*
- Song: "Don't Get Around Much Anymore"

- Artist: Maynard Ferguson Orchestra
- Recording: *Just a Memory*
- Song: "Frame for the Blues"

Beginning Improvisation Ensemble—*Oceans*

Description

The goal of this exercise is to draw inspiration from physical phenomena to create a range of dynamics and to understand the strong connections musicians and listeners make between dynamics and the musical elements of timbre, rhythm, and melody. Students are then challenged to break associations such as loud is fast, and quiet is slow and are encouraged to explore other compositional devices that express dynamic levels.

Materials

- Projector and/or computer screen.
- Images of sunrises, ocean waves, tornadoes.
- Silent films of downslope skiing, skydiving.
- Pulsating images from screensavers.
- Ruler or laser pointer.
- Recording device.

Learning Goals

- Students will musically interpret a visual image or silent film about a physical phenomenon.
- Students will identify what parts of an image imply certain levels of dynamics.

- Students will change associations they make between loud and soft dynamics with other compositional devices.

Procedure

- The teacher points to a visual image (or shows a silent film) depicting a physical phenomenon and students begin to play with dynamics that reflect the level of tension within the image. Students should also be encouraged to explore various timbres on their instruments and melodic/rhythmic motives as they musically express the image. If the students are not comfortable providing their own melodic/harmonic material, the teacher can provide a musical color palette in the form of a designated scale or even a limited pitch set of four to five pitches.
- The teacher slowly moves the pointer to different points of the image (or plays the film) and students change dynamics, timbre, rhythm, and melodic devices accordingly.
- The teacher drags the pointer to a final resting point off the screen (or concludes the silent film) to bring the piece to an end.
- The students and the teacher discuss how certain parts of the image had tension, while others may have depicted release. The teacher should connect how the concept of tension and release relates to dynamics.
- As a class they should consider the following: What timbres and melodic/rhythmic devices were used when we performed *ff*? What timbre and melodic/rhythmic devices were used when we performed *pp*? For example, if all loud sections were played with fast rhythms, and quiet sections were played with slow elongated rhythms, the teacher should challenge students to do the opposite for a dynamic level, or students should change the timbre, or melodic motif for that section.
- The students should perform the image again and discuss as a class how the performance of the piece differed from the first time through.

Assessment

Formative

- The teacher records each performance and posts the performances along with the image or video to a class discussion board. The teacher asks students to choose one of the recordings and describe how it is a strong depiction of the image.

Summative

- The teacher asks each student to choose one of the class recordings and write a reflection on how he used melody, rhythm, or timbre to support the dynamics and the musical interpretation of the image. Students are assessed on their detail of explanation in relation to the image and recording. Students are also assessed on the variety of musical techniques they are able to explain within their own performance.

Lesson Benefits

- Students identify tension and release in dynamics.
- Students identify and explore the relationships between dynamics and melodic/rhythmic devices as well as timbre.
- Students musically interpret a physical phenomenon as many composers have done over the centuries and across genres.

Images

Artist: Michael Clark
Pieces: Landscape photography

Artist: Walter De Maria
Piece: *The Lightning Field*

Artist: Sebastião Salgado
Pieces: Landscape photography

Artist: Claude Monet
Pieces: Haystack series

Artist: Diego Rivera
Piece: *Cantina*

Artist: Vincent van Gogh
Piece: *Starry Night*

Intermediate Improvisation Ensemble—*Studio Magic*

Description

This lesson blends improvisation with a composition style many refer to as "musique concrète" or the experimental usage of sounds that were not originally intended for musical purposes. For the purpose of this activity, these sounds can include incidental everyday sounds such as a car horn or sounds intentionally created by the student such as tapping fingernails on a desk. These sound effects often evoke unique dynamic gestures that can inform creative dynamic improvisations. Such sound effects should be collected in a "sound-effect bank" and then layered as part of a sonic texture in a music production program. This collection gives an individual or group the opportunity to improvise over a unique, often non-tonal, sound-effect texture. *Note: This lesson is different from "Imitation of Found Sounds" in that "Studio Magic" specifically prompts students to digitally record and collect the sounds, if technologically possible.*

Materials

- Recording technology.
- Music production software.

Learning Goals

- Students will observe and imitate the unique dynamic gestures of incidental sound effects in their improvisations.
- Students will use composition and improvisation to develop distinct sonic textures.
- Students will musically assess the timbre and textural possibility of different "sound effects" as part of a larger musical blend.
- Students will experiment with improvising over non-tonal textures and recorded loops.
- Students will learn to use recording technology and music production software to enhance the creative process.

Procedure

- The teacher should prompt the students to record sounds that are not intended for musical purposes. The sounds can be external sounds, including those produced by nature (e.g., a dog barking) or not (e.g., a car horn in traffic). The students can also feel free to personally create sound effects as they do in movie studios. An example of this effect might be the sound of stepping on a bed of pebbles. If the students need inspiration for this task, this video link is a wonderful example of how sound artists create effects in a Hollywood movie studio: https://www.youtube.com/watch?v=UO3N_ PRIgX0&t=315s.
- Without regard for what sounds are selected, the teacher should compile a "sound bank" of these sounds with an identical file format (e.g., MP3). *Note: If the teacher/students cannot record sound effects themselves, there are many websites such as* zapsplat. com *that feature free, downloadable, public domain sound effects.*
- The next step is for the teacher to put students in groups. Each group will be assigned a composition activity of inserting sounds from the "sound bank" into a music production program such as GarageBand or Audacity. The goal is for each group to create at least one minute of a sound-effect "texture" or "quilt." Other than the length, there are no rules for the sonic nature of the texture. The students produce an identical repeating texture for the duration of the excerpt or feature a variety of interweaving sounds and textures.
- The final step is for the teacher or students to create a digital recording of a group's excerpt and challenge students to perform either a solo or group improvisation over the recorded sonic texture.
- The non-tonal nature of this particular format lends itself to a more abstract, less formal improvisation approach for students. Students should be encouraged to experiment freely by imitating the unique timbre and dynamic gestures of the sound effects.

- *Note the following two items:*
  1. If the teacher/students have access to a synthesizer, guitar pedals, or a particular digital tablet application, this activity can be a particularly fun exploration of different sound effects.
  2. If the teacher and/or students wish to perform the activity but do not have access to recording technology, computers, or music production software, they can use the format of "Found Sounds" to facilitate the activity. It should be noted, however, that this approach requires one group of students to create a steady texture of sounds while an individual or group improvises over that sonic texture.

Assessment

Formative

- A group of students record themselves improvising over the created sonic texture and informally reflect on different possibilities for the performance format.
- Students can be invited to identify or bring in examples of film sound effects in which the dynamic gesture and/or timbre effectively propels the film's narrative. This video clip is a fun example of movie studio sound effects that can provoke student thought on this issue.
- Students can creatively attempt to *produce* different sound effects in a similar approach as that of movie studio sound technicians.

Summative

- Students write a reflection on their improvised sound effects by imagining a scene that would align with the sequence. Students should also describe why the music effects (dynamics, texture, and timbre) made them imagine the scene. The teacher assesses whether students are able to use the music elements of dynamics, texture, and timbre to support their imagined plot. Students can view the video clip link as an example of how Hollywood creates movie sound effects: https://www.youtube.com/watch?v=UO3N_PRIgX0&t=315s

Lesson Benefits

- Students can learn to conceptualize and listen to group texture and timbre within the context of dynamics.
- Students can creatively weave a sonic texture based on various sound effects.
- Students can learn to use recording technology and music production software to enhance their creative music making.

Recordings

Please visit the Oxford University Press Companion Website for three different versions (Listening Examples 11.1–11.3 ⊙) of this activity as performed by the Lane Technical High School theory class.

- Artist: Miles Davis
- Recording: *Bitches Brew*

- Artist: The Mothers of Invention/Frank Zappa
- Recording: *We're Only in It for the Money*

- Artist: Fred Frith
- Recording: *Speechless*

- Artist: Steven Price
- Recording: *Gravity* (original motion picture soundtrack)

- Artist: Vangelis
- Recording: *Blade Runner* (original motion picture soundtrack)

- Artist: Branford Marsalis
- Recording: *I Heard You Twice the First Time*
- Song: "Berta, Berta"

- Composer: Edgar Varèse
- Recording: *Varèse: The Complete Works*

SECTION IV

Portals of Discovery

Vignettes in Improvisation
Teaching and Learning

Introduction

We believe that by engaging students in the types of lessons that we have presented in the previous section, they will discover their musical "spontaneous selves." They will feel and apply aspects of their musicianship that are uncomfortable and at first may feel wrong, but through these experiences they will come to know, reframe, and refine their musicianship in ways that were previously not possible. As they listen, respond, play, engage, and give of themselves through creative expression they will tumble and fall, and you, as the teacher, have to be there to catch them and help them get up again. Through these experiences you and your students will have new determination and focus in your large ensemble and class music making.

It can be difficult to imagine how these lessons may play out in a real-life context, particularly since the teaching and learning of improvisation in K–12 settings beyond jazz ensembles is still relatively uncommon (Hickey, 2012). In this section, we provide vignettes of our lessons to help you visualize the reasons, contexts, responses, and outcomes of engaging in improvisation activities. These vignettes are based on our experiences teaching improvisation to students in K–12, collegiate, and workshop settings. They exemplify the types of knee-jerk reactions musicians feel when they are challenged to think, hear, and perform in ways that they have not experienced before, but they also personify the musical growth that comes out of these experiences. The vignettes are also written in a way to help educators imagine how they might incorporate these activities, given the realistic time constraints on day-to-day schedules.

Beginning Instrumental/Choral Ensemble— *"Indie in D" for Middle School Concert Band*

Mr. Kelly directs a very successful middle school band program. His groups have excellent enrollment, they consistently give high-quality performances, and most of his students really enjoy participating in band. Even though everybody in the district and community is happy with Mr. Kelly's work, he had begun to yearn for something more. In particular, he wanted to add some more creative musical activities to the students' experience. At the time, he was not entirely sure where to start. Improvisation activities seemed like a bit of a long shot. Mr. Kelly had almost no jazz experience. His primary instrument was the oboe, and the jazz ensembles did not feature oboe players in his high school days. His district hired a part-time jazz ensemble director so that Mr. Kelly could focus exclusively on the large band program. Before he started working as a full-time band director, he enjoyed arranging band and marching band music but he has not really had time to do that since he started teaching.

After some deliberation, Mr. Kelly decided on an approach that combined elements of composition and improvisation. He had always been a fan of minimalist music, particularly the works of Terry Riley and Steve Reich. He decided to have his advanced eighth-grade students perform Terry Riley's *In C* in their lesson sectionals. *In C* consists of a series of musical fragments in the key of C. Musicians are expected to perform a series of composed melodic fragments, starting whenever each musician prefers, and repeating each fragment as many times as each musician wants. The students mostly seemed to enjoy playing *In C*, particularly because there was no pressure on them other than to decide how many times to play each fragment. After doing this activity for about a month, the students started to get a little bored with that particular piece. It occurred to Mr. Kelly that the students typically have little or no trouble playing in the key of C major. Recently, however, they started playing a difficult band piece in the key of E♭ major that was giving the band some trouble. Mr. Kelly decided to embrace the broad concept of *In C* by compiling some of the challenging melodic fragments from the difficult concert band piece. In sectionals, he presented them with the melodic fragments and gave them the same protocol as Riley's *In C*. Although they were apprehensive at first, the students began to enjoy the activity because it let them repeat certain fragments as many times as they wished, creating a thicker linear texture where individual note "flubs" did not stand out. Some students also began to develop interest in the different ensemble textures produced by the same collection of fragments and tried to alter the overall texture by playing the fragments in different ways over each performance.

Beginning Instrumental/Choral Ensemble—"Nontraditional Sounds" for Middle School Chorus

Ms. Gibson was excited to work on Bob Chilcott's arrangement of *Mari's Wedding* with her middle school chorus. The tune required light and lively singing, but more importantly, would address some of the rhythmic weaknesses the group had been graded down for in the previous year's assessment. The piece featured the Scotch snap throughout the melody, and an intricate offbeat clapped accompaniment. Her goal was to familiarize students with the syncopated sixteenth-and eighth-note combination, but not to spoon-feed them the rhythms for accuracy. Instead, she wanted them to take ownership of understanding the intricacies of the rhythms.

At the beginning of her Monday rehearsal, she quietly began chanting rhythms including the Scotch snap, moving from simple to more complex patterns. But rather than simply chant them on "bah," she used her body and her voice in nontraditional ways to capture the crisp short-long features of the rhythm. She snapped, slid, and used "vizz" and "ah" nonsense syllables, just to name a few. Students had never seen her engage in this type of music-making, and understandably, there were giggles and questioning looks as she started the process. But as they heard her get into a groove, they quieted. At the end of her chant, there was quiet and then applause. Little did they know that they would be tasked with creating similar sounds at home!

Ms. Gibson asked the students to open *Mari's Wedding* and she highlighted three challenging rhythms within the work. Their assignment was to go home and find nontraditional sounds with their voices or bodies for each of the three rhythms, practice the rhythms until they felt the rhythms were accurate, and then record and upload them to the class website. She explained that her goal was to see if they could accurately perform the rhythms while they were thinking about how sounds and articulations of sounds lend to the crispness of certain rhythms. Students murmured disapproval at the idea, but Ms. Gibson piqued their curiosity further by saying that some of their ideas would be used in further group performances. Ms. Gibson assured them that their recordings would remain private, and this exploration into sound would be made public with others only if they chose to share their sounds in class. This assurance seemed to satisfy her middle school choristers and they went home to practice rhythm in ways they had never thought of before.

Students were given three days to practice and record their rhythms. As recordings began to roll in, Ms. Gibson was amazed at the creative thought students put into sound selections that highlighted the intricacies of the rhythms. There were pops, lip smacks, ranges of sound, and nonsense syllables that she could have never imagined herself. What was even more interesting was how students worked through the rhythms! Some would ground their performances over a steady beat of a foot tap or snap, and others attempted to put two or more of the rhythms together at the same time. This is the very thing she wanted to attempt with them in class! Students were demonstrating an even deeper level of understanding of the rhythms without her asking! She was excited and motivated to see where the in-class improvisations would take them in the next rehearsal.

Beginning Improvisation Ensemble—*"Oceans" for Elementary General Music*

Ms. Jackson's fifth grade music class had developed a clear understanding of texture, form, and timbre, and could perform melody and rhythm with accuracy. She knew that they had the musical "know-how" for ensemble performances in middle school. However, performing with vitality was not something they had quite achieved. They were good at following the guidelines, even basic conducting gestures, but they did not seem to listen for or understand the intricacies of balance and expression. Ms. Jackson wanted to prepare them to be engaged and responsive musicians.

In early November, as the weather shifted and coolness settled in, she decided to mix things up. Her fifth grade classes entered a dark room with an image of lightning engaging with Walter De Maria's sculpture *The Lightning Field*. They were quietly instructed to choose a classroom instrument at the front of the room and to take a seat at their spot. Students could choose instruments ranging from Orff instruments that they were accustomed to using, to instruments that had traditionally been kept more hidden in the back, like the vibra slap. It was an interesting array of possibilities, and as students looked at the mood of the image, they sometimes returned to the front, choosing something different.

Ms. Jackson's opening instructions were quite simple: "Welcome to class today. Thank you for quietly choosing an instrument and taking your seat. We are going to perform the image you see before you. I will point to a starting place and you will use your instrument in a way that captures the feeling of the image at that point. I will move my pointer across the image, just as if you were reading a piece of music, and you will depict the sounds that best capture it. Please show me you are performance ready."

Students immediately rose to their knees, mallets in performance position and strikers at optimal striker distance, to play what they believed to be the most tenuous part of the image—the lightning! But Ms. Jackson did not take them there. She started on the gray-blue clouds to the right of the screen, watching and listening to their response. Despite this quieter part of the image, some students still excitedly dove in. She noticed others playing back, tentatively trying to find the right sounds on the instruments she had provided. She had an appreciation for the contrasts in their energy. Her goal was for them to see and hear the way they were conceiving this image, and to work together to solve this imaginative score.

At the end, she asked a simple question: "What did you notice about your performance?" Hands flew in the air: "We were loud at the lightning, almost too loud for my ears!" "We slowed down as we came back to the blue-gray clouds." "We played really low in the darkest parts of the image." "We were all playing at the lightning part." So many wonderful observations for Ms. Jackson to go on! She quickly realized that these types of conversations were just the beginning of her students' uncovering the intricate relationships between dynamics, texture, range, timbre, and so much more. Upon seeing their excitement and closing the activity for the day in rich reflective dialogue, she strategized ways to pace out this lesson in the coming weeks and to build on the relationships between dynamics, timbre, texture, and range through improvisatory and compositional activities for the rest of the year.

Intermediate Improvisation Ensemble—"Techno Music" for Secondary General Music

Mr. Vasquez had begun the year with a new secondary general music class added to his schedule. To be honest, he was not enthralled with the prospect of teaching such a wide variety of students from across the school. Differences in their musical backgrounds were vast. Some students had never been in a music class before in their lives! Where would he begin? Normally, he taught high school band, which was a much different format from this setting.

The premise of the class was to be a music appreciation class for non-performance students, but Mr. Vasquez was invited to structure it however he wanted. He decided that exploring the musical elements of melody, harmony, rhythm, texture/timbre, articulation, and dynamics could be the best approach to this particular class. He was a teacher who believed strongly in the "doing" of music. However, how was he going to get the students to "do" if they had not played before? On the basis of student interest sheets, he knew that they were avid listeners of music, primarily current popular music. If he could get them to lean on their aural understandings, he believed he could get them to do music and to explore the elements with meaning.

He had a small inventory of instruments ranging from tubano drums and tambourines, to a few Orff xylophones and broken-stringed ukuleles. He put all into working order, and ventured into his first music-making experience with his class of twenty-two ninth- and tenth-grade students. He decided to build on their interests of dance and techno music and had them listen to songs by Amon Tobin. He conceptually lectured on ideas of texture and articulation, but also invited students to identify how many rhythmic layers happened over repeating basslines.

In the next week, he introduced the undulating half-step bassline of *Foam* from Tobin. Students were invited to stand and tap out the beat in their feet or hands. Mr. Vasquez had inputted the bassline into GarageBand and let it loop continuously. The gut instinct of most students was to imitate the subdivision present in the bassline, but as they watched and listened to one another they all began to settle into the beat. Mr. Vasquez began to snap a two-bar ostinato over it, and then gestured for the students to take it over. He moved into another pattern in his feet, and gestured for half of the class to take over that pattern. He watched and listened until both patterns settled like clockwork and then quietly walked over to the volume and faded out the recording. This was his demonstration of what was to come.

For the next lesson they were to create layers like a grid, with different articulations through instruments and voice, and fit it all on top of the bassline from *Foam*. As he introduced their role to them, he saw their faces light up and he realized that the creative "doing" of articulation had changed their skeptical moods from just a week prior into excitement and determination. He was now even more committed to connecting every musical element discussed in the course to creative music making.

Intermediate Jazz Ensemble—"Flamenco Mittens With String" for High School Jazz Ensemble

Ms. Hall was getting her high school jazz ensemble ready for a concert about a month away. She was mostly happy with the band's progress but, as usual, she was much more satisfied with the students' progress playing ensemble parts than improvising. In fact, she planned every semester with the hope of working on improvisation more and it just never seemed to work out. Ms. Hall herself was mostly versed in classical trumpet, but she had taken the time to read up on jazz theory and listened to big band jazz regularly. The problem did not seem to be her own musical expertise; it was that there was just too much that the students did not know when it came to jazz improvisation, particularly playing chord changes. She gave the students chord/scale relationship exercises and prompted the students to perform the arpeggios as scales over the chord changes in their jazz repertoire, but it never sounded even close to organic. Unlike with her wind ensemble, in which the more difficult repertoire was mainly an extension of the students' existing technique, when it came to jazz improvisation there was so much that the students flat out did not know: modal harmony, chord/scale relationships, jazz phrasing, organic eighth-note swing. This gulf of knowledge along with the need to rehearse the section parts usually led her to "give up" and tell the students to improvise over a pentatonic or blues scale.

Vowing not to fall back on her "safety plan" this time, Ms. Hall decided to change the format of the solo chord changes. She took out a jazz piece that mainly featured ii–V⁷–I progressions. She selected a particular ii–V⁷–I in the key of F and instructed the rhythm section to vamp on the G minor seventh chord. Alone and in groups she encouraged the students to explore that G minor chord. She reminded them that G Dorian is the scale most commonly used over that chord but encouraged them to just explore the "sound" on their instruments. When they had done so over all three chords of the progression, she invited soloists to improvise over the progression with the rhythm section, except the student musicians were instructed to switch to the next chord whenever they were ready, using body language to indicate a harmony switch. Many students were very reluctant to participate, so Ms. Hall would ask them to participate in the activity as part of a group improvisation so that they could explore and experiment without a solo spotlight on anxious students. After two weeks, she could already hear a difference in the students' improvisations. They were no longer struggling to keep track of where they were in fast-moving chord changes. They were also soloing much more melodically, whereas before they almost always started each scale on the root position in their solos. Most importantly, they were really listening and aurally perceiving the harmonies instead of keeping track visually.

As it came around to concert time, the students were still not ready to improvise over a series of ii–V⁷–I chords at tempo, but Ms. Hall thought, "Why not?" She asked them to perform their solos at the concert the same way that they practiced the activity in class. Although the students were not performing the chord changes exactly as written (in a rhythmic sense), the solos sounded much more organic and melodic at this concert. The parents and the rest of the audience also seemed to perceive that the students were less "panicky," and many approached her after the concert to let her know that they really enjoyed the student solos.

Intermediate Instrumental/Choral Ensemble—
"Middle Eastern Taqsim" for High School Orchestra

Mr. Fox's high school orchestra had been struggling with intonation issues on various minor scales and also experienced difficulty with nuanced rubatos in his conducting of Glasunov's *Theme and Variations*. He decided to take a step back and approach the beauty of minor tonalities in a new light. One day as students entered the classroom, he had the oud music of Rahim Alhaj playing in the background. Students took out their instruments and looked quizzically at one another. Mr. Fox challenged them to quietly find the tonic and drone with the recording. At the end of the recording, he asked the students to find the scale that most closely aligned with patterns they had heard in the recording, and to play quietly up and down the scale at a pace that suited them. What he noticed in his students was intense listening, slow bowing, rich tone, and relaxed playing. That was his introduction to taqsim for the day.

The next time students arrived, Mr. Fox encouraged them to warm up again in a similar fashion but on the D natural minor scale. He had a new guideline for them: to repeat, hold, and pause on each note of the scale, playing the scale ascending and descending in a sequential order. He droned for them by grabbing a nearby cello, and everyone safely moved up and down the scale, coming to a close at different times. He then asked students to partner up, and drone for each other while the other repeated the activity. Students were to listen to each other and comment on the emphases that they heard and the quality of their tone. This individualized attention between peers was new, and a bit unnerving for some. But Mr. Fox let peers choose partners, giving them agency in their vulnerability. The room first filled with nervous chatter, and then as students leaned into the music making, beautiful sonorities filled the room. After students droned for each other and commented on each other's performance, they were invited back to their orchestra seats. Mr. Fox invited them to pull out Glasunov's *Theme and Variations*. He could feel an immediate difference in their listening and responses to the melodic lines throughout the work. He decided to continue the improvisational teaching in the subsequent days.

Two days later at the start of rehearsal, a few of the students began to ask whether they would be playing scales over drones again. What they had not even realized is that they were indeed improvising! Mr. Fox wondered if he should even point this out. Some of the students seemed so enthralled with the relaxing approach to rehearsal that they had not noticed how creative and flexible they were becoming in their playing. He decided to roll out the new guideline: Students should begin to create small motifs that could be sequenced up and down the scale. At first students seemed bothered by this new stipulation, and sequencing was certainly not something they did regularly when practicing scales! Mr. Fox chose to put himself out there to demonstrate sequencing over the minor scale. Students had never heard him play freely away from the music. He began simply and freely playing a sequence on D, F, E, D, E, D. Then he moved this idea up again on

E and F. He then slowly and freely returned to the tonic, using repetition, and paused to bring all listeners closer to the tonic. His students were enraptured as they listened to him combine ideas from the previous day with sequence. Mr. Fox ended and felt a different connection with his students—a closeness and focus that was rarely achieved in rehearsal. He knew it was because he had demonstrated his own vulnerabilities in a new and different musical style. Students saw beauty in his tone, and possibility in his simple and approachable example. They split into pairs, and again engaged in a reflective and creative endeavor.

Mr. Fox continued with these exercises over the next few weeks, layering in new guidelines, listening to pertinent examples, and relating the freedom in their playing to the repertoire they were working on in rehearsal. As he provided new guidelines, students sometimes bemoaned the new challenges. They were unsure of the ornamentation and aspects of musicality. To keep up their momentum, Mr. Fox encouraged them to always start from a place where they were comfortable with the taqsims. Not everything had to be mastered at one time. He also posted recordings for them to listen to, and he encouraged them to pick out just one aspect of the ornamentations—perhaps small flipped grace notes, slides, or just sequenced patterns in one section. The permission to limit their focus on these aspects seemed to free them again in their playing. As he continued to include taqsim activities in his rehearsals, he was amazed at the focus these exercises brought to students' musical engagement. He was also thrilled to hear students carrying these ideas into their own personal practice!

Epilogue

We sincerely hope that you are able to incorporate a few of these lessons into your ensembles or classrooms. We have attempted to describe activities with enough routes and options so that you can work these activities into your existing music curriculum. That being said, the lessons described in this book obviously will not anticipate every eventuality in your music class. If we can offer a final suggestion, it is that you stay as flexible as possible. The inherent beauty of teaching musical improvisation is that both teaching and music improvisation require quite a bit of flexibility. Just as you will encounter a new "take" on notes, harmonies, and rhythms every time that you improvise, you will never have a group of students identical to the students who are sitting right in front of you.

As we have stated earlier in this book, it is perfectly normal for a music teacher to feel anxious if he or she does not have extensive improvisation experience. The good news is that, as a music teacher, you are quite likely already using flexible and creative teaching approaches, maybe not for improvisation activities per se, but perhaps for choir warm-ups, marching band drills, or Orff lessons in the general music classroom. This same pedagogical flexibility will be invaluable when you are trying the lessons in this book. We are constantly in awe of the dedication, flexibility, and creativity demonstrated by music teachers around the world. We hope that music teachers, ranging from improvisation experts to novices, will take the suggested activities in this volume and flexibly use them in their own personal approach with their unique group of students in mind. Good luck and have fun!

References

Ankney, K. L. (2014). *Master jazz teachers' noticing and responses to students during improvisation activities* (Doctoral dissertation). Retrieved from Proquest Dissertations and Theses (UMI 3669190).

Bailey, D. (1992). *Improvisation: Its nature and practice in music.* Boston, MA: Da Capo Press.

Berkman, D. (2007). *Conceptual scores for large ensemble.* Unpublished manuscript.

Berliner, P. F. (1994). *Thinking in jazz: The infinite art of improvisation.* Chicago, IL: University of Chicago Press.

Bernhard, H. C. (2013). Music education majors' confidence in teaching improvisation. *Journal of Music Teacher Education, 22*(2), 65–72.

Bernhard, H. C., & Stringham, D. A. (2016). A national survey of music education majors' confidence in teaching improvisation. *International Journal of Music Education, 34*(4), 383–390.

Borgo, D. (2007). *Free jazz in the classroom: An ecological approach to music education.* San Diego, CA: UC San Diego Previously Published Works.

Buber, M. (1957). *Between man and man.* Boston, MA: Beacon Press.

Csikszentmihalyi, M. (1991). *Flow: The psychology of optimal experience.* New York, NY: Harper & Row.

Duke, R. A. (2005). *Intelligent music teaching: Essays on the core principles of effective instruction.* Austin, TX: Learning and Behavior Resources.

Eisner, E. (2002). *The arts and the creation of mind.* New Haven, CT: Yale University Press.

Greene, M. (1978). Teaching: The question of personal reality. *Teachers College Record, 80*(1), 23–35.

Hammer, D., Goldberg, F., & Fargason, S. (2012). Responsive teaching and the beginnings of energy in a third grade classroom. *Review of Science, Math, and ICT Education, 6*(1), 51–72.

Healy, D. (2014). "Play it again, Billy, but this time with more mistakes": Divergent improvisation activities for the jazz ensemble. *Music Educators Journal, 100*(3), 67–72.

Hickey, M. (2009). Can improvisation be 'taught'? A call for free improvisation in our schools. *International Journal of Music Education, 27*(4), 285–299.

Hickey, M. (2012). *Music outside the lines: Ideas for composing in K–12 music classrooms.* New York, NY: Oxford University Press.

Juster, N. (1961). *The phantom tollbooth.* New York, NY: Alfred A. Knopf.

Lebowitz, F. (1981). *Social studies.* New York, NY: Random House.

Lee, L. Y. (1986). *Rose.* Rochester, NY: BOA Editions.

Lisk, E. (1991). *Alternative rehearsal techniques: The creative director.* Delray Beach, FL: Meredith Music.

Morris, B. (2017). *The art of conduction: A conduction® workbook.* New York, NY: Karma.

Nachmanovitch, S. (1991). *Free play: Improvisation in life and art.* New York, NY: Penguin Putnam.

Norgaard, M. (2016). Unlocking your potential as an improviser. *American String Teacher, 66*(2), 26–29.

Oliveros, P. (2005). *Deep listening: A composer's sound practice*. Lincoln, NE: Deep Listening Publications.

Pugatch, J. (2006). *Acting is a job: Real-life lessons about the acting business*. New York, NY: Allworth Press.

Rowe, M. (2010, October 3). A wrong note? [Blog post]. Retrieved from http://jazzbackstory.blogspot.com/2010/10/wrong-note.html

Rowling, J. K. (1997). *Harry Potter and the sorcerer's stone*. New York, NY: Scholastic.

Sarath, E. (1996). A new look at improvisation. *Journal of Music Theory, 40*(1), 1–38.

Sawyer, K. (2004). Creative teaching: Collaborative discussion as disciplined improvisation. *Educational Researcher, 33*(2), 12–20.

Schopp, S. E. (2006). A study of the effects of National Standards for music education, number 3, improvisation and number 4, composition on high school band instruction in New York State (Doctoral dissertation). Retrieved from Proquest Dissertations and Theses (UMI 3225193).

Spolin, V. (1999). *Improvisation for the theater: A handbook of teaching and directing techniques*. Evanston, IL: Northwestern University Press.

Stake, R. E. (1973, October). Program evaluation: Particularly responsive evaluation. Paper presented at New Trends in Evaluation, Göterburg, Sweden.

Sudnow, D. (1978). *Ways of the hand: The organization of improvised content*. Cambridge, MA: MIT Press.

Zarour, W. (2012, September). *Middle Eastern taqsim*, Old Town School of Folk Music, Chicago, IL.

RESOURCE REFERENCES

Compositions

Bedford, D. (1974). *12 hours of sunset* [Score]. New York, NY: Universal Edition.

Berlioz, H. (1830/2006). *Symphonie fantastique, Op. 14* [Score]. Mainz, Germany: Schott Music.

Brahms, J. (1877/2010). *Symphony no. 2* [Score]. Mainz, Germany: Schott Music.

Britten, B. (1945). *Peter Grimes* [Score]. London, UK: Boosey & Hawkes.

Copland, A. (1944/2004). *Appalachian spring* [Score]. London, UK: Boosey & Hawkes.

Gershwin, G. (1924/1942). *Rhapsody in blue* [Score]. New York, NY: Warner Bros.

Glinka, M. (1842/1969). *Russlan and Ludmilla* [Score]. New York, NY: Muzyka.

Holst, G. (1916/1997). *The planets* [Score]. Mineola, NY: Dover Publications.

Ives, C. (1935). *Three places in New England* [Score]. Boston, MA: C. C. Birchard.

Ives, C. (1907, later revised/1953). *The unanswered question* [Score]. St. Louis, MO: Southern Music.

Ligeti, G. (1966/2002). *Lux aeterna* [Score]. Leipzig, Germany: Edition Peters.

Orff, C. (1936/1981). "O fortuna" from *Carmina Burana* [Score]. Mainz, Germany: Schott Music.

Ravel, M. (1929). *Boléro* [Score]. Bryn Mawr, PA: Theodore Presser.

Reich, S. (1973). *Music for pieces of wood* [Score]. New York, NY: Universal Edition.

Riley, T. (1964). *In C* [Score]. Los Angeles, CA: G. Schirmer and Associated Music Publishers.

Sousa, J. P. (1889). *The thunderer* [Score]. Public domain.

Sousa, J. P. (1889). *The Washington Post* [Score]. Public domain.

Sousa, J. P. (1893). *The Liberty Bell* [Score]. Public domain.

Sousa, J. P. (1896). *The stars and stripes forever!* [Score]. Public domain.

Stockhausen, K. (1968). *Stimmung* [Score]. New York, NY: Universal Edition.

Stravinsky, I. (1913/1933). "Augurs of spring" in *The Rite of Spring* [Score]. New York, NY: Kalmus.

Stravinsky, I. (1954). *In memoriam Dylan Thomas: Dirge canons and song for tenor, string quartet, and four trombones* [Score]. London, UK: Boosey & Hawkes.

Tchaikovsky, P. I. (1892/1987). *The Nutcracker suite* [Score]. Mineola, NY: Dover Publications.

Tchaikovsky, P. I. (1876/1997). *Swan Lake* [Score]. Mineola, NY: Dover Publications.

Vivaldi, A. (1725/1995). "Allegro non molto" from *Violin concerto in G minor (summer) RV 315* [Score]. Mineola, NY: Dover Publications.

Wagner, R. (1865/1973). *Tristan und Isolde* [Score]. Mineola, NY: Dover Publications.

Wagner, R. (1870/1978). *Die Walküre* [Score]. Mineola, NY: Dover Publications.

Wagner, R. (1876/1982). *Götterdämmerung* [Score]. Mineola, NY: Dover Publications.

Wagner, R. (1876/1983). *Siegfried* [Score]. Mineola, NY: Dover Publications.

Wagner, R. (1869/1985). *Das Rheingold* [Score]. Mineola, NY: Dover Publications.

Films

Cuarón, A., & Heyman, D. (Producers), & Cuarón, A. (Director). (2013). *Gravity* [Motion picture]. United States: Warner Bros. Pictures.

Disney, W., & Sharpsteen, B. (Producers), & Alger, J., Armstrong, S., Beebe, F., Ferguson, N., Hand, D., Handley, J., Hee, T., Jackson, W., Luske, H., Roberts, B., Satterfield, P., & Sharpsteen, B. (Directors). (1940). *Fantasia* [Motion picture]. United States: Walt Disney Productions.

Kubrick, S., & Lyndon, V. (Producers), & Kubrick, S. (Director). (1968). *2001: A space odyssey* [Motion picture]. United States: Metro-Goldwyn-Mayer.

Phillips, J., & Phillips, M. (Producers), & Spielberg, S. (Director). (1977). *Close encounters of the third kind* [Motion picture]. United States: Columbia Pictures.

Thomas, E., Nolan, C., & Obst, L. (Producers), & Nolan, C. (Director). (2014). *Interstellar* [Motion picture]. United States: Paramount Pictures.

Online Videos

[Alvin Ailey American Dance Theater]. (2016, December 28) [Video file]. *"Revelations" by Alvin Ailey.* Retrieved from https://www.youtube.com/watch?v=tNqaixKbrjs

[Bidoujess]. (2007, May 23). *Spontaneous inventions—Bobby McFerrin* [Video file]. Retrieved from https://www.youtube.com/watch?v=5VfyMPHzYdQ

[Casa Patas, flamenco en vivo]. (2018, June 25). *Casa Patas, flamenco en vivo #303—Antonio Canales, Bailaor* [Video file]. Retrieved from https://www.youtube.com/watch?v=IhwwWfhAYWQ

[ducu bertzi]. (2013, February 7). *Bobby McFerrin demonstrates the power of the pentatonic scale* [Video file]. Retrieved from https://www.youtube.com/watch?v=SZEjUhJ_nPc

[Great Big Story]. (2017, January 12). *The magic of making sound* [Video file]. Retrieved from https://www.youtube.com/watch?v=UO3N_PRIgX0&t=315s

[HubbardStreetDance]. (2015, March 2). *Hubbard Street Dance Company in "Cloudless" by Alejandro Cerrudo* [Video file]. Retrieved from https://www.youtube.com/watch?v=iEgcff5020Q

[Martha Graham Dance Company]. (2016, April 28). *Martha Graham in Lamentation* [Video file]. Retrieved from https://www.youtube.com/watch?v=I-lcFwPJUXQ

[National Arab Orchestra]. (2013, September 1). *Michigan Arab Orchestra: Cello taqsim—Naseem Alatrash* [Video File]. Retrieved from https://www.youtube.com/watch?v=9_z4jKdVINc

[Sadler's Wells Theatre]. (2014, February 18). *Farruquito—Improvisao—Sadler's Wells is dance* [Video file]. Retrieved from https://www.youtube.com/watch?v=rNc7aXApUdA

[Tunes04]. (2008, May 29). *Crazy (Gnarls Barkley cover)—Ray LaMontagne* [Video file]. Retrieved from https://www.youtube.com/watch?v=6mEfDSP4g_U

Recordings

Ainger. (2013). *Shatter* (Marc Ainger, composer) (fixed media) [Sound File]. Retrieved from https://soundcloud.com/ainger/shatter

Albert, J. (2013). *The tree on the mound* [CD]. Paris, France: RogueArt.

Alhaj, R. (Oud). (2006). Taqsim maqām bayyat husayni. On *When the soul is settled: Music of Iraq* [CD]. Washington, DC: Smithsonian Folkways.

Barkley, G. (2008). Crazy. On *St. Elsewhere* [CD]. London, United Kingdom: Warner Brothers.

Basie, W., & Foster, F. (1959). Blues in Hoss' flat [Recorded by the Count Basie Orchestra]. On *Chairman of the board* [CD]. New York, NY: Roulette Records.

Basie, W. (2000). *Count Basie—Ken Burns jazz* [CD]. Santa Monica, CA: Verve Records.

Bengtsson, E. B. (1995). *Johann Sebastian Bach: 6 solo suites* [CD]. Copenhagen, Denmark: Danacord Records.

Berling, T. (2013). *True* [Recorded by Avicii] [CD]. London, United Kingdom: Island Records.

Bill Holman Band. (1995). *A view from the side* [CD]. New York, NY: Victor Entertainment.

Bloom, J. I. (1992). *Art & aviation* [CD]. New York, NY: Arabesque.

Blount, H. P. (1959). *Jazz in silhouette* [Recorded by Sun Ra and his Arkestra] [CD]. Chicago, IL: El Saturn Records.

Blount, H. P. (1974). *Space is the place* [Recorded by Sun Ra and his Arkestra] [CD]. Conshohocken, PA: Evidence Music.

Blount, H. P. (1978). *Languidity* [Recorded by Sun Ra and his Arkestra] [CD]. Philadelphia, PA: Philly Jazz.

Braxton, A. (1976). 22-M, opus 58. On *Creative orchestra music 1976* [CD]. Santa Clara, CA: Arista Records.

Brickman, J. (2012). *Piano lullabies* [CD]. East Aurora, NY: Fisher-Price.

Brubeck, D. (1953). *Jazz at Oberlin* [CD]. Los Angeles, CA: Fantasy Records.

Brubeck, D. (1959). *Time out* [CD]. New York, NY: Columbia Records.

Burton, G., & Corea, C. (1973). *Crystal silence* [CD]. Munich, Germany: ECM Records.

Byron, D. (1996). *Bug music* [CD]. New York, NY: Nonesuch Records.

Casals, P. (2012). *J. S. Bach: Six solo suites for cello* [CD]. New York, NY: Warner Classics.

Chemical Brothers. (1995). *Exit planet dust* [CD]. London, United Kingdom: Virgin Records.

Cleaver, G. (2007). 6350. On *Gerald Cleaver's Detroit* [CD]. Barcelona, Spain: Fresh Sound New Talent.

Cobain, K. (1992). Come as you are [Recorded by the Charlie Hunter Trio]. On *bing, bing, bing!* [CD]. New York, NY: Blue Note Records. (1995)

Coleman, O., & Kühn, J. (1997). *Colors: Live From Leipzig* [CD]. New York, NY: Harmolodic/Verve.

Cujo. (1996). *Adventures in Foam*. London, England: Ninebar Records.

Daft Punk. (2001). *Discovery* [CD]. New York, NY: Virgin Records.

Davis, M. (1959). Flamenco sketches [Recorded by the Miles Davis Sextet]. On *Kind of blue* [CD]. New York, NY: Columbia Records.

Davis, M. (1969). *In a silent way* [CD]. New York, NY: Columbia Records.

Davis, M. (1970). *Bitches brew*. New York, NY: Columbia Records.

Deep Listening Band. (2017). Section II: Lapis lazuli. On *Dunrobin sonic gems*. Retrieved from https://paulineoliveros1.bandcamp.com/album/dunrobin-sonic-gems

DeJohnette, J. (1976). Sorcery no. 1 [Recorded by the John Abercrombie Trio]. On *Gateway* [CD]. Munich, Germany: ECM Records.

Donelian, A. (2002). *Grand ideas, volume 2: Mystic heights* [CD]. New York, NY: Sunnyside Records.

Dorham, K. (1963). Blue bossa [Recorded by the Joe Henderson Quintet]. On *Page one* [CD]. New York, NY: Blue Note Records.

Ellington, E. (1937/1956). Diminuendo and crescendo in blue [Recorded by the Duke Ellington Orchestra]. On *Ellington at Newport* [CD]. New York, NY: Columbia Records.

Ellington, E. (1940). Don't get around much anymore [Recorded by Louis Bellson and Explosion]. On *Note smoking* [record]. Oxnard, CA: Voss Records. (1988)

Fitzgerald, E., & Armstrong, L. (1956). *Ella and Louis* [CD]. Santa Monica, CA: Verve Records.

Fleck, B., Hussein, Z., & Meyer, E. (2009). *The melody of rhythm* [CD]. Port Washington, NY: Koch.

Frisell, B. (2000). What a world, under a golden sky, winter always turns to spring [Recorded by Bill Frisell]. On *Ghost town* [CD]. New York, NY: Nonesuch Records.

Frith, F. (1980). *Gravity* [CD]. San Francisco, CA: Ralph Records.

Frith, F. (1981). *Speechless* [record]. San Francisco, CA: Ralph Records.

Gabriel, P. (1986). Mercy street [Recorded by Peter Gabriel]. On *So* [CD]. London, United Kingdom: Virgin Records.

Gershwin, G., & Gershwin, I. (1930). I've got rhythm [Recorded by the Don Byas/Slam Stewart Duo]. On *Smithsonian collection of classic jazz, volume 3* [CD]. Washington, DC: Smithsonian.

Gershwin, G., Heyward, D., & Gershwin, I. (1959). Prayer. On *Porgy and Bess* [Recorded by Miles Davis and Gil Evans] [Record]. New York, NY: Columbia Records.

Gould, G. (2002). *Glenn Gould: A state of wonder—The complete Goldberg Variations 1955 & 1981* [CD]. New York, NY: Sony Classical.

Green, F. (1957). Corner pocket [Recorded by the Count Basie Orchestra]. On *April in Paris* [Record]. Santa Monica, CA: Verve Records.

Hahn, H., & Hauschka. (2012). *Silfra* [CD]. Berlin, Germany: Deutsche Grammophon.

Hampton, L. W. (1958). Frame for the Blues [Recorded by the Maynard Ferguson Orchestra]. On *Just a memory* [CD]. Montreal, Canada: Just A Memory Records, Inc. (1996)

Hampton, L., Goodman, B., & Robin, S. (1939). Flyin' home [Recorded by Lionel Hampton and his Orchestra]. On *Flyin' home: The best of the Verve years* [CD]. Santa Monica, CA: Verve Records. (1994)

Hancock, H. (1965). *Maiden voyage* [Record]. Englewood Cliffs, NJ: Blue Note Records.

Henderson, R., & Dixon, M. (1957). Bye, bye blackbird [Recorded by the Miles Davis Quintet]. On *Round about midnight* [Record]. New York, NY: Columbia Records.

Henderson, R., & Dixon, M. (1959). Bye, bye blackbird [Recorded by Ben Webster/Oscar Peterson]. On *Ben Webster meets Oscar Peterson* [Record]. Santa Monica, CA: Verve Records.

Henderson, R., & Dixon, M. (1966). Bye, bye blackbird [Recorded by the Clark Terry/Bob Brookmeyer Quintet] On *Gingerbread men* [Record]. New York, NY: Mainstream Records.

Herman, W., & Bishop, J. (1939). Woodchopper's ball [Recorded by the Woody Herman Orchestra]. On *The best of Woody Herman* [CD]. Nashville, TN: Curb Records. (2011)

Holman, B. (1995). *A view from the side* [CD]. Yokohama, Japan: JVC.

Jarrett, K. (1975). *The Köln concert* [Record]. Munich, Germany: ECM Records.

Jarrett, K. (1999). *The melody at night, with you* [CD]. Munich, Germany: ECM Records.

Jazz Mandolin Project. (2003). Pointillism. On *Jungle tango* [CD]. Burlington, VT: Lenapee Records.

Johnson, N. (2012). *Looper* (Original motion picture soundtrack) [CD]. Burbank, CA: La-La Land Records.

Julyan, D. (2001). *Memento* (Original motion picture soundtrack) [CD]. New York, NY: Sire Records.

Julyan, D. (2002). *Insomnia* (Original motion picture soundtrack) [CD]. Beverly Hills, CA: Varèse Sarabande.

Julyan, D. (2006). *The descent* (Original motion picture soundtrack) [CD]. London, United Kingdom: Cooking Vinyl.

Limón, J. (2018). Promesas de tierra [Recorded by Javier Limón]. On *Promesas de tierra* [CD]. Brookline, MA: Casa Limón America.

Lovano, J. (1995). Fort Worth [Recorded by the Joe Lovano Quartet]. On *Quartets: Live at the Village Vanguard* [CD]. New York, NY: Blue Note Records.

Lovano, J., & Schuller, G. (1994). *Rush hour* [CD]. New York, NY: Blue Note.

Machito. (1961). *Machito at the Crescendo* [Record]. Detroit, MI: Vogue Records.

Marsalis, B. (1992). Berta, Berta. On *I heard you twice the first time* [CD]. New York, NY: Sony Records.

Marsalis, B. (1999). Lykief. On *Requiem* [CD]. New York, NY: Columbia Records.

McCartney, P., & Lennon, J. (1966). Eleanor Rigby [Recorded by Stanley Jordan]. On *Magic touch* [CD]. Los Angeles, CA: Blue Note Records. (1985)

Mingus, C. (1959). *Mingus ah um* [Record]. New York, NY: Columbia Records.

Mingus, C. (1960). *Blues & roots* [Record]. New York, NY: Atlantic Records.

Mingus, C. (1993). *Mingus Big Band 93: Nostalgia in Times Square* [Recorded by the Mingus Big Band] [CD]. Paris, FR: Dreyfus Records.

Mitchell, J. (1969). Both sides now. On *Clouds* [Record]. New York, NY: Reprise Records.

Mitchell, J. (2000). Both sides now. On *Both sides now* [CD]. New York, NY: Warner.

Monk, T. S. (1957). Brilliant corners. On *Brilliant corners* [Record]. New York, NY: Riverside Records.

Monk, T. S. (1963). *Monk's dream* [Record]. New York, NY: Columbia Records.

Monk, T. S. (1965). *Solo Monk* [Record]. New York, NY: Columbia Records.

Montero. G. (2008). *Baroque* [CD]. Paris, France: Warner Classics.

Morris, L. D. (1991). *Dust to dust* [CD]. New York, NY: New World Records.

Motian, P. (1977). Trieste [Recorded by the Keith Jarrett Quartet]. On *Byablue* [Record]. New York, NY: Impulse! Records.

Motian, P. (1985). It should've happened a long time ago [Recorded by the Paul Motian Trio]. On *It should've happened a long time ago* [CD]. Munich, Germany: ECM Records.

Motian, P. (2004). *I have the room above her* [CD]. Munich, Germany: ECM Records.

Okazaki, M. (2006). *Mirror* [CD]. New York, NY: Released independently.

Oliveros, P., Dempster, S., & Panaiotis. (1989). Lear. On *Deep listening* [CD]. San Francisco, CA: New Albion.

Oliveros, P., Dempster, S., & Panaiotis. (1989). Suiren. On *Deep listening* [CD]. San Francisco, CA: New Albion.

Parker, C. (1951). Au privave [Recorded by Charlie Parker]. On *Bird's best bop on Verve* [Record]. Santa Monica, CA: Verve Records.

Parks, A. (2008). *Invisible cinema* [CD]. New York, NY: Blue Note Records.

Potts, B. (1967). Big swing face [Recorded by the Buddy Rich Big Band]. On *Big swing face* [Record]. Los Angeles, CA: Pacific Jazz Records.

Price, S. (2013). *Gravity* (Original motion picture soundtrack) [CD]. Burbank, CA: WaterTower Music.

Prima, L. (1936). Sing, sing, sing [Recorded by the Benny Goodman]. On *Live at Carnegie Hall* [Record]. New York, NY: Columbia Records. (1950)

Propellerheads. (1998). *Decksandrumsandrockandroll* [CD]. London, United Kingdom: Wall of Sound.

Rodgers, R., & Hammerstein, O. (1959). My favorite things [Recorded by the John Coltrane Quartet]. On *My favorite things* [Record]. New York, NY: Atlantic Records. (1961)

Rodgers, R., & Hammerstein, O. (1943/1952). People will say we're in love [Recorded by 1952 studio cast]. On *Oklahoma!* [Record]. New York, NY: Sony Classical.

Rollins, S. (1956). Blue 7 [Recorded by Sonny Rollins]. On *Saxophone colossus* [Record]. Hackensack, NJ: Prestige.

Schneider, M. (1996). Coming about [Recorded by the Maria Schneider Orchestra]. On *Coming about* [CD]. Munich, Germany: Enja Records.

Scott, R. (1998). *The music of Raymond Scott: Reckless nights and Turkish twilights* [CD]. Aalsmeer. The Netherlands: Basta Music.

Silver, H. (1965). Song for my father [Recorded by the Horace Silver Quintet]. On *Song for my father* [Record]. Englewood Cliffs, NJ: Blue Note Records.

Shankar, R. (1962). *Improvisations* [Record]. New York, NY: Angel Records.

Shankar, R. (1973). *Live in 1972* [Record]. London, UK: Apple Records.

Shorter, W. (1968). Nefertiti [Recorded by the Miles Davis Quintet]. On *Nefertiti* [Record]. New York, NY: Columbia Records.

Stalling, C. (2012). *The Carl Stalling Project—Music from Warner Bros. cartoons 1936–1958 by The Carl Stalling Project* [CD]. New York, NY: Warner Brothers.

Stepanyan, A. (Duduk). (2002). Quail. On *Ancient lands: Traditional dudek music from Armenia* [CD]. West Bloomfield, MI: American Recording Productions.

Stevens. S. (2010). Vesuvius. On *Age of Adz* [CD]. Holland, MI: Asthmatic Kitty.

Styne, J., & Cahn, S. (1944). I guess I'll hang my tears out to dry [Recorded by the Dexter Gordon Quartet]. On *Go* [Record]. New York, NY: Blue Note Records (1962)

Tizol, J. (1941). Perdido [Recorded by the Dave Brubeck Quartet]. On *Jazz at Oberlin* [Record]. Los Angeles, CA: Fantasy Records. (1953)

Tower of Power. (2001). *The very best of Tower of Power: The Warner years* [CD]. New York, NY: Warner/ Rhino.

Townshend, P. (1971). Baba O'Riley [Recorded by The Who]. On *Who's next* [Record]. London, United Kingdom: Track Records.

Townshend, P. (1971). Won't get fooled again [Recorded by The Who]. On *Who's next* [Record]. London, United Kingdom: Track Records.

Vangelis. (1994). *Blade runner* (original motion picture soundtrack)[CD]. New York City, NY: Atlantic Records.

Varèse, E. (1998). *The complete works:* [Recorded by Royal Concertgebouw Orchestra/Asko Ensemble] [CD]. London, England: Decca Records.

Waldron, M. (1957). Soul eyes [Recorded by the Joel Frahm Quartet]. On *Sorry, no decaf* [CD]. Redding, CT: Palmetto Records. (2005)

Waller, T. W. (1928). Willow tree [Recorded by the Vanguard Jazz Orchestra]. On *Monday night live at the Village Vanguard* [CD]. Catskill, NY: Planet Arts Recordings. (2008)

Webster, B. (1962). Better go [Recorded by the Ben Webster/Harry "Sweets" Edison Quintet]. On *Ben and "Sweets"* [Record]. New York, NY: Columbia Records.

Werner, K. (2001). *Form and fantasy* [CD]. Paris, France: Night Bird Music.

Wheeler, K. (1976). *Gnu high* [Record]. Munich, Germany: ECM Records.

Whitacre, E. (2010). *Light & gold* [CD]. London, United Kingdom: Universal Music Operations Limited.

Williams, J. (1977). *Close encounters of the third kind* (original motion picture soundtrack) [Record]. Santa Clara, CA: Arista Records.

Winter, P. (1985). *Canyon* [CD]. Litchfield, CT: Living Music.

Young, L. (2000). *Lester Young—Ken Burns jazz* [CD]. Santa Monica, CA: Verve Records.

Zimmer, H. (2014). *Interstellar* (original motion picture soundtrack) [CD]. Burbank, CA: WaterTower Music.

Zorn, J. (2000). *Cartoon/S&M* [CD]. New York, NY: Tzadik.

Visual Arts

Clark, M. (2019, July 31). *Michael Clark Photography*. Retrieved from https://www.michaelclarkphoto.com/

de Kooning, E. (1959). *Bullfight* [oil on canvas]. Denver Art Museum, Denver, CO.

de Kooning, E. (1960). *Bullfight* [acrylic on paper]. Modern Museum of Art (MoMA), New York, NY.

De Maria, W. (1977). *Lightning field* [sculpture]. Dia Art Foundation, Quemado, NM.

Frankenthaler, H. (1952). *Mountains and sea* [oil and charcoal on canvas]. National Gallery of Art, Washington, DC.

Kandinsky, W. (1916). *Moscow: Red Square* [oil on canvas]. State Tretyakov Gallery, Moscow, Russia.

Lewis, N. (1948). *Jazz band*. Retrieved from https://arthive.com/artists/73639~Norman_Lewis/works/487274~Jazz_band

Marin, J. (1932). *Region of Brooklyn Bridge fantasy* [watercolor, colored pencil, and graphite pencil on paper]. Whitney Museum of Modern Art, New York, NY.

Monet, C. (1891). *Stacks of wheat (end of day, autumn)* [oil on canvas]. Art Institute of Chicago, Chicago, IL.

Monet, C. (1891). *Stacks of wheat (end of summer)* [oil on canvas]. Art Institute of Chicago, Chicago, IL.

Pollock, J. (1949). *Untitled (green silver)* [enamel and aluminum paint on paper, mounted to canvas]. Guggenheim, New York, NY.

Pollock, J. (1954). *White light* [oil, enamel, aluminum paint on canvas]. Museum of Modern Art (MoMA), New York, NY.

Rivera, D. (1937). *Cantina* [watercolor, gouache, and black ink on Japan paper]. Maximilian Contemporary, Oakland, CA.

Salgado, S. (2019, July 31). *Sebastião Salgado*. Retrieved from https://www.artsy.net/artist/sebastiao-salgado

Van Gogh, V. (1889). *The starry night* [oil on canvas]. Modern Museum of Art (MoMA), New York, NY.

Index